Shadows in the water: Supporting refugees in their homelands

DM Ole Kiminta

Published by DM Ole Kiminta, 2024.

SHADOWS IN THE WATER: SUPPORTING REFUGEES IN THEIR HOMELANDS

First edition. October 9, 2024.

ISBN: 979-8227437440

Written by DM Ole Kiminta.

Table of Contents

Chapter 1: Shadows in the water

Supporting refugees in their homelands
Crossing the Mediterranean Sea

There have been questions asked by many about why certain individuals especially Africans have taken dangerous journeys of crossing Mediterranean Sea. There are no straight answers for these questions unless we look at the real cause and reasons behind this migration to European countries.

Refugees are individuals who are forced to flee their home countries due to persecution, armed conflict, or violence. The 1951 Refugee Convention defines a refugee as someone who has a well-founded fear of being persecuted for reasons of race, religion, nationality, membership in a particular social group, or political opinion. This definition underscores the complex realities that drive people to seek asylum across international boarders. Understanding who qualifies as a refugee is essential for creating effective policies and support systems that address their needs and circumstances.

The context in which refugees emerge is often marked by instability and hardship. Many refugees originate from regions afflicted by war, political turmoil, or systemic discrimination. For instance, countries in the Middle East and North Africa have witnessed significant upheaval, particularly in the wake of the Arab Spring and subsequent conflicts. These crises not only displace individuals but also create environments where basic human rights are compromised, further exacerbating the urgency for safe havens. Recognising this backdrop is crucial for comprehending the motivations behind mass migrations and the challenges faced by those who leave their countries.

The post-World War II era marked a significant shift in the global approach to displacement, with the establishment of international frameworks aimed at protecting the rights of refugees. The 1951 Refugee Convention and its 1967 Protocol laid the groundwork for international cooperation in addressing the needs of displaced persons. This legal framework emerged in response to the atrocities of the war, emphasizing the importance of providing sanctuary to those fleeing persecution. However, while these instruments aimed to create safe havens, they also highlighted the limitations of existing systems, often failing to address the root causes of displacement, which continue to drive individuals to seek refuge elsewhere.

In the context of the Mediterranean, historical factors such as colonial legacies and geopolitical tensions have played a critical role in shaping migration patterns. Countries in North Africa and the Middle East have faced various forms of instability, from authoritarian regimes to civil wars, prompting many to flee in search of safety. The Arab Spring, for instance, triggered mass movements of people escaping violence and oppression, leading to a surge in refugees attempting to reach Europe. Understanding these historical contexts is vital in recognising that displacement is not merely a contemporary phenomenon but a continuation of long-standing struggles for safety and dignity.

The Mediterranean Sea has become a focal point for refugee movements, particularly as many seek refuge in Europe. The perilous journey across this body of water is often undertaken by those escaping dire situations in their home countries. Tragically, many do not survive the journey, highlighting the urgent need for international intervention and support. The context of the Mediterranean crossing is not just about physical displacement; it involves social, economic, and cultural dimensions that must be understood to foster empathy and effective assistance for refugees.

Addressing the plight of refugees requires a multifaceted approach that includes both immediate humanitarian aid and long-term strategies for stabilisation in their countries of origin. Initiatives aimed at improving conditions in refugee home countries can play a significant role in reducing the need for mass migration. By investing in infrastructure, education, and governance, the international community can help create environments where individuals feel safe and valued, thus empowering them to remain in their own countries rather than embark on dangerous journeys across boarders.

Dangers of the Journey

The journey undertaken by refugees seeking safety and a better life often involves perilous routes, with the Mediterranean Sea being one of the most treacherous. Many embark on this journey due to a combination of conflict, persecution, and dire economic conditions in their home countries. The dangers they face are not merely physical; they encompass a range of psychological and emotional challenges that can have long-lasting effects on individuals and families. Understanding these risks is crucial for developing effective support systems that address the root causes of displacement and help prevent such journeys from occurring in the first place.

One of the most immediate dangers of crossing the Mediterranean is the risk of drowning. Overcrowded and unseaworthy vessels are frequently used by smugglers, leaving refugees vulnerable to capsizing or sinking. Many refugees are not skilled swimmers, and the panic that ensues during emergencies can exacerbate the situation. Tragically, thousands have lost their lives in these waters, and the fear of death looms large over those who choose to embark on this journey. This stark reality underscores the need for policies and interventions that provide safe, legal pathways for migration and prevent the reliance on dangerous routes.

In addition to the physical dangers, refugees often face exploitation and abuse while in transit. Smugglers, who prey on the desperation of those fleeing conflict, may subject individuals to violence, extortion, and trafficking. Women and children are particularly vulnerable in these situations, facing a heightened risk of sexual violence and exploitation. The trauma endured during the journey can leave deep psychological scars, complicating the already challenging process of rebuilding lives in a new country. Addressing these issues requires a comprehensive understanding of the motivations behind migration and the vulnerabilities that arise during the journey.

The journey can also lead to significant health risks. Refugees may travel for days or weeks with limited access to food, clean water, or medical care, resulting in malnutrition and illness. The stress and uncertainty of the journey can exacerbate pre-existing health conditions or lead to new ones, including mental health issues such as anxiety and depression. Health services in transit countries are often inadequate, further complicating the situation for those in need. By investing in health infrastructure and services in refugees' home countries, the international community can help mitigate these health risks and support individuals in staying safe and healthy.

Ultimately, the dangers of the journey highlight the urgent need for collective action to address the underlying causes of forced migration. By focusing on humanitarian aid, conflict resolution, and economic development in refugees' home countries, we can create conditions that reduce the necessity for such perilous journeys. Efforts to support refugees in their homelands not only save lives but also foster stability and resilience within communities. As we seek to create a world where individuals are not forced to flee their homes, understanding and addressing these dangers is an essential step in the journey toward a more equitable and compassionate global society.

Overview of Migration Routes

Migration routes have historically been shaped by a multitude of factors including conflict, economic opportunities, and environmental changes. This complexity is evident in the various paths taken by refugees seeking safety and stability. Among these routes, the journey across the Mediterranean Sea to Europe has garnered significant attention due to its perilous nature and the humanitarian crises it often entails. Understanding these migration routes is essential for recognizing the challenges refugees face and for exploring viable solutions that might allow them to remain in their homelands.

The Mediterranean migration route is characterised by its diverse origins and destinations. Many refugees originate from countries plagued by violence, persecution, or extreme poverty, such as Syria, Afghanistan, and sub-Saharan African nations. These individuals and families often embark on dangerous journeys, risking their lives in search of safety and a better future. The Mediterranean Sea serves as a critical juncture, with various embarkation points in North Africa, particularly Libya and Tunisia, leading to destinations in southern Europe, including Italy and Greece. This journey is fraught with challenges, including human trafficking, overcrowded vessels, and the constant threat of drowning.

The motivations behind these migration routes are influenced by both push and pull factors. Push factors, such as armed conflict, human rights violations, and economic instability, compel individuals to flee their homes. Conversely, pull factors, including perceived safety and opportunity in European countries, entice them to undertake the dangerous crossing. The interplay of these factors creates a complex web of migration patterns, where individuals weigh the risks of their journey against the potential for a safer and more prosperous life.

Addressing these underlying issues is crucial for developing effective interventions aimed at supporting refugees.

In response to the ongoing migration crisis, various international organisations and governments have sought to implement policies aimed at managing migration flows and providing humanitarian assistance. Initiatives such as search and rescue operations in the Mediterranean, as well as resettlement programs, have been established to mitigate the risks associated with the journey. However, these measures often fall short of addressing the root causes of migration. To truly support refugees, it is essential to focus on creating conditions that enable individuals to thrive within their own countries, rather than relying solely on migration as a solution.

In conclusion, the overview of migration routes, particularly the perilous journey across the Mediterranean Sea, highlights the urgent need for comprehensive strategies that prioritize support for refugees in their homelands. By addressing the factors that drive individuals to migrate, fostering stability, and promoting economic opportunities, the international community can work towards a future where individuals do not feel compelled to leave their homes in search of safety. Ultimately, enhancing the conditions within refugees' countries of origin will not only reduce the need for dangerous migrations but also contribute to global stability and human dignity.

The origins of African migration, particularly in the context of crossing the Mediterranean, can be traced back to a complex interplay of historical, economic, and social factors. Migration from Africa has occurred for millennia, driven by a combination of environmental changes, population pressures, and the search for better opportunities. The earliest migrations were often in search of fertile land and resources, as communities moved in response to climatic shifts and the availability of water. Over time, these movements evolved, influenced by trade routes and the expansion of empires.

By the 15th century, the dynamics of migration began to change dramatically with the rise of the transatlantic slave trade. European powers established trade networks that forcibly transported millions of Africans across the Atlantic to work in plantations and mines. This brutal system not only led to significant loss of life and culture but also contributed to the destabilization of various African societies. As communities were torn apart, many sought refuge and new beginnings by migrating northward across the Mediterranean, aiming to escape the violence and disruption caused by the slave trade.

In the modern context, the situation has morphed into a reckless to almost suicidal daring emigrating to Europe by many individuals. We therefore witness a new wave of people who try to change their lives in a hurry by heading North to cross the Mediterranean Sea while some come from Asia, Arab countries, and many from sub-Saharan countries.

Migration across the Mediterranean has taken on new dimensions, influenced by political instability, economic hardship, and climate change. Countries in North Africa, particularly Libya and Tunisia, have become focal points for migrants attempting to reach Europe. The allure of better economic prospects and safety from conflict drives many to undertake perilous journeys across the sea. This contemporary migration reflects a continuation of historical patterns, with individuals and families seeking to improve their circumstances in the face of adversity.

Understanding the origins of African migration enhances our comprehension of the current migration crisis across the Mediterranean. It is essential to recognise

that these movements are not merely a result of recent events but rather rooted in centuries of historical experiences. By examining the past, we can better appreciate the complexity of migration today and the ongoing struggles faced by those who risk everything for a chance at a better life. The narrative of African migration is a testament to resilience, shaped by a long history of searching for safety, opportunity, and hope.

The scramble for Africa in the late 19th century, characterised by European colonization and competition, further influenced migration patterns. European powers divided the continent without regard for existing ethnic and cultural boundaries, which led to the displacement of numerous communities. As colonial administrations imposed new economic structures and labor systems, many Africans were coerced into migrating to urban centers or plantations to meet the demands of European economies. This forced migration created a new class of labourers who were often exploited and marginalised, setting the stage for future migrations that would continue long after the colonial period.

World War II was another pivotal moment that shaped migration trends. The conflict resulted in widespread upheaval and destruction across Europe and North Africa, prompting many Africans to seek refuge or new opportunities in Europe. The post-war era saw a demand for labor in rebuilding efforts, leading to the recruitment of Africans into European labour markets. This period of migration was complex, as it was driven by both the need for economic stability in Europe and the aspirations of Africans seeking better lives. The legacies of colonialism and war intertwined, creating a dynamic landscape of migration that would continue to evolve in the following decades.

The contemporary migration crisis across the Mediterranean is deeply rooted in the historical events that preceded it. Economic instability, political unrest, and the legacies of colonialism have driven many Africans to embark on perilous journeys across the sea in search of safety and opportunity. The ongoing conflicts in countries like Libya and Syria, coupled with the effects of climate change, have exacerbated the situation, forcing individuals and families to flee their homes. Understanding the historical context of these migrations is essential for grasping the complexities of the current crisis, as it reveals the enduring impacts of past injustices and the human desire for freedom and a better future.

The Mediterranean's significance in the transference of knowledge and culture cannot be overstated. As Africans crossed its waters, they brought with them rich traditions, languages, and beliefs, which influenced the cultures of Europe and the Mediterranean basin. These interactions contributed to the development of multicultural societies, enriching the artistic and intellectual heritage of the region. However, the narratives of those who crossed the Mediterranean under duress often remain marginalized. Recognizing and amplifying these voices is essential to understanding the full complexity of Mediterranean history and the enduring legacies of slavery.

Today, the Mediterranean continues to be a site of migration and a symbol of hope and despair. The ongoing journeys of individuals seeking refuge or a better life echo the historical movements of Africans across this sea. Understanding the historical importance of the Mediterranean is crucial for contemporary discussions about migration, identity, and cultural heritage. It provides a lens through which we can examine the legacies of the past, fostering a deeper appreciation for the interconnectedness of human experiences across time and space.

Environmental Challenges Faced by Migrants

Environmental challenges faced by migrants crossing the Mediterranean are multifaceted and significant. Climate change has had a profound impact on the African continent, resulting in increased desertification, erratic rainfall patterns, and heightened frequency of extreme weather events. These environmental changes have led to diminished agricultural productivity, forcing many people to abandon their homes in search of more viable living conditions. As traditional livelihoods become unsustainable, communities are left with little choice but to migrate, often undertaking perilous journeys across the Mediterranean.

Water scarcity is another pressing environmental challenge that exacerbates the displacement of populations. Many regions in Africa are experiencing severe water shortages, which not only affect drinking water supplies but also limit agricultural irrigation. This scarcity drives competition for resources, leading to conflict and instability in some areas. As families and individuals find their access to clean water increasingly threatened, many are compelled to leave their homes in search of more stable environments, often leading them to the Mediterranean route with the hope of reaching Europe.

The degradation of ecosystems also plays a significant role in the migration crisis. Deforestation, soil erosion, and loss of biodiversity undermine the resilience of communities that rely on natural resources for their survival. As these ecosystems deteriorate, food security becomes a pressing issue, further fueling the decision to migrate. Many migrants embark on their journeys with the hope of escaping environmental degradation that has rendered their home regions unlivable, only to face additional challenges upon reaching the Mediterranean.

Moreover, the journey across the Mediterranean itself poses significant environmental hazards. Migrants often travel in overcrowded and unseaworthy vessels, which are vulnerable to the unpredictable conditions of the sea. The risk of capsizing, drowning, and exposure to harsh weather is a constant threat. Additionally, many migrant routes are littered with environmental hazards such as pollution and debris, further complicating an already dangerous journey. These environmental challenges not only endanger the lives of the migrants but also highlight the broader implications of environmental degradation in their home countries.

Finally, the intersection of environmental challenges and migration underscores the urgent need for comprehensive strategies that address the root causes of displacement. Efforts to combat climate change, promote sustainable development, and enhance local resilience are critical in mitigating the environmental factors driving migration. By addressing these issues, the international community can help create conditions that allow people to thrive in their home countries, reducing the need for treacherous journeys across the Mediterranean and ultimately curbing the cycle of migration that leads to vulnerability and exploitation.

Chapter 3: The Drivers of Migration

Economic Factors

The economic factors influencing the migration of Africans across the Mediterranean are deeply intertwined with historical, social, and political contexts. For centuries, the economies of many African nations have been shaped by colonialism and the exploitation of natural resources. The legacy of these practices has created systemic poverty and economic instability, pushing individuals and families to seek better opportunities elsewhere. The allure of Europe, often viewed as a land of prosperity and opportunity, becomes a beacon for those trapped in dire economic circumstances.

One of the primary economic drivers of migration is the disparity in employment opportunities between Africa and Europe. In many African countries, high unemployment rates, particularly among the youth, exacerbate the struggle for a better life. The lack of jobs often leads to desperation, prompting individuals to embark on perilous journeys across the Mediterranean in search of work. Many believe that reaching European shores will provide access to a more stable job market, higher wages, and improved living conditions, despite the inherent risks involved in such a journey.

Additionally, economic policies and practices in both Africa and Europe contribute to the migration crisis. Structural adjustments imposed by international financial institutions have often led to cuts in social services and public spending in African nations, further entrenching poverty. Simultaneously, Europe's labour market demands often remain unfulfilled, creating a paradox where migrants are needed yet simultaneously vilified. This demand for labour in sectors such as agriculture, construction, and hospitality contrasts sharply with the experiences of migrants, who often face exploitation and discrimination upon arrival.

The role of remittances also plays a significant part in the economic factors surrounding migration. Many migrants who successfully reach Europe send money back home to their families, providing essential support that can alleviate poverty and improve living conditions. This financial lifeline reinforces the idea that migration can lead to economic improvement, encouraging further migration as families seek to secure a better future through these remittances. However, this reliance on migrant income can also create a cycle where families become dependent on the economic contributions of those abroad, perpetuating the desire to migrate.

Understanding these economic factors is crucial for comprehending the broader context of African migration across the Mediterranean. Addressing the root causes of economic disparity, improving job opportunities, and fostering local economies are essential steps toward alleviating the pressures that drive individuals to undertake such dangerous journeys. By recognising the complex interplay of factors that influence migration, policymakers, educators, and communities can work towards creating sustainable solutions that honor the dignity and aspirations of those seeking a better life.

Political Instability and Conflict

Political instability in North Africa has been a significant factor contributing to the perilous journeys of many Africans crossing the Mediterranean in search of better opportunities. Countries such as Libya, Tunisia, and Egypt have experienced varying degrees of political turmoil over the past decade. The aftermath of the Arab Spring in 2011 led to power vacuums, weak governance, and the rise of militant groups, particularly in Libya. These conditions have created environments where human rights are often violated, and individuals are driven to flee their homes under dire circumstances, hoping for safety and stability in Europe.

Conflict plays a crucial role in exacerbating the challenges faced by migrants. In regions where civil wars and sectarian violence prevail, such as in parts of Syria and South Sudan, individuals are forced to leave their countries to escape violence and persecution. This push factor is compounded by the lack of economic opportunities in their home nations. As conflicts continue, the number of people seeking refuge and a better life in Europe rises, often leading them to undertake treacherous sea journeys that can result in tragic outcomes.

The smuggling networks that have emerged in response to this crisis thrive in regions of political instability. These networks exploit the desperation of those fleeing conflict, charging exorbitant fees for unsafe passage across the Mediterranean. Many migrants find themselves at the mercy of ruthless smugglers who often abandon them in perilous situations. The lack of effective law enforcement and the chaotic political landscape make it challenging for governments to combat these criminal enterprises, further endangering vulnerable populations.

International responses to political instability and conflict in Africa have varied, but often fall short of addressing the root causes of migration. While organisations may provide humanitarian assistance, the underlying issues—such as governance failures, economic disparities, and ongoing violence—remain unaddressed. Consequently, the cycle of instability continues, perpetuating the conditions that force individuals to risk their lives on dangerous migratory routes. Efforts to stabilise regions are essential to create environments where individuals can live without fear of conflict or persecution.

Understanding the relationship between political instability, conflict, and migration is crucial for developing comprehensive solutions. Educational institutions, libraries, and universities play an important role in fostering dialogue and awareness around these issues. By studying the complexities of migration and the factors that drive it, society can work toward informed policies that not only address immediate humanitarian needs but also promote long-term stability and peace in affected regions. The journeys across the Mediterranean are not just tales of desperation; they are also stories that reflect the broader geopolitical landscape of Africa and the profound human desire for safety and opportunity.

Climate Change and Environmental Degradation

Climate change represents one of the most urgent challenges facing humanity today, with profound implications for the environment and human societies. In the context of Africa, where many communities depend heavily on natural resources for their livelihoods, the impacts of climate change are particularly acute. Rising temperatures, changing precipitation patterns, and increasing frequency of extreme weather events disrupt agricultural practices, threaten food security, and exacerbate existing vulnerabilities. These environmental changes create a ripple effect, intensifying social and economic pressures that can drive migration, including the perilous journeys across the Mediterranean in search of a better life.

Environmental degradation, fueled by climate change, further compounds these challenges. Deforestation, desertification, and the degradation of water resources reduce the resilience of ecosystems and the communities that depend on them. In many African regions, unsustainable agricultural practices and industrial activities contribute to the loss of biodiversity and the deterioration of land quality. As ecosystems collapse, communities are left with limited options, often forcing individuals and families to migrate in search of more favorable living conditions. This migration is not merely a quest for economic opportunity; it is often a desperate response to the loss of a sustainable way of life.

The journey across the Mediterranean is fraught with danger and uncertainty, a reflection of the extreme conditions that trigger such migration. For many Africans, the decision to embark on this perilous voyage is driven by a combination of environmental factors, including droughts and floods that disrupt their homes and livelihoods. These environmental stressors can lead to a sense of hopelessness, pushing individuals to undertake treacherous crossings in search of safety and stability. As they navigate the complexities of migration, these individuals often face exploitation and abuse, highlighting the urgent need for policies that address the root causes of migration while ensuring the protection of vulnerable populations.

International responses to climate change and environmental degradation must take into account the specific challenges faced by African nations. Coordinated efforts are needed to enhance adaptive capacity, promote sustainable development, and mitigate the impacts of climate change. This includes investing in renewable energy, improving agricultural practices, and restoring degraded ecosystems. By addressing these environmental challenges, there is potential not only to reduce the pressures that lead to migration but also to empower communities to thrive in their home environments. The integration of climate action into migration policies can create frameworks that protect the rights and dignity of migrants while fostering sustainable development.

The relationship between climate change, environmental degradation, and migration is complex and multifaceted, particularly in the context of the Mediterranean crossings. Understanding this dynamic is essential for educators, policymakers, and communities engaged in addressing the challenges faced by Africans seeking better futures. By fostering awareness and promoting informed dialogue, it is possible to build resilience against climate impacts, support sustainable migration pathways, and ultimately contribute to a more just and equitable world. The stories of those who embark on these journeys serve as a reminder of the urgent need for collective action in the face of environmental and humanitarian crises.

Chapter 4:

The Journey Begins
Departure Points in Africa

The journey of Africans across the Mediterranean has its roots in various departure points across the continent, each with its unique historical, cultural, and socio-economic contexts. These departure points are not merely geographical locations; they represent the complex tapestry of human experience, resilience, and the harsh realities faced by individuals seeking better lives. The coastal regions of North Africa, particularly Libya, Tunisia, and Egypt, have become significant hubs for migration due to their proximity to Europe. These areas have historically been influenced by trade, conflict, and colonial legacies, which have shaped the patterns of movement across the Mediterranean.

Libya stands out as a pivotal departure point, often described as a gateway to Europe. Over the years, political instability and civil conflict have transformed Libya into a transit country for thousands of migrants. Many of these individuals embark on perilous journeys, driven by the desire to escape poverty, violence, and persecution in their home countries. The Mediterranean Sea, while representing hope and opportunity, also embodies danger and uncertainty, as countless migrants have tragically lost their lives in the attempt to cross its waters. The Libyan coast has become synonymous with the harrowing experiences of those who seek to navigate these treacherous routes.

Tunisia, located just a short distance from the Italian island of Lampedusa, has also emerged as a significant departure point. The 2011 Arab Spring and subsequent socio-economic challenges have led to increased migration from Tunisia. Historically, this country has been a melting pot of cultures and influences, which has fostered a spirit of resilience among its people. Many Tunisians, along with migrants from sub-Saharan Africa, view the crossing as a chance for a new beginning. However, the realities of the journey often clash with the aspirations of those who embark on it, as they confront the risks associated with overcrowded boats and unscrupulous smugglers.

Egypt, with its long coastline along the Mediterranean, is another critical departure point for migrants. The country's unique geopolitical position makes it a transit hub for individuals fleeing conflict and economic hardship from countries like Sudan, Eritrea, and Somalia. The migration patterns from Egypt reflect broader trends in the region, where individuals seek safety and stability. Nevertheless, the journey from Egypt is fraught with challenges, including human trafficking and exploitative conditions. The experiences of migrants from this region highlight the intersection of desperation and hope, as they navigate the complexities of their journeys.

The departure points in Africa showcase the diverse motivations and challenges faced by those crossing the Mediterranean. While these locations may be defined by their geographical coordinates, they are imbued with the stories of individuals who carry the weight of their aspirations, fears, and histories. Understanding these departure points is essential for comprehending the broader narrative of migration across the Mediterranean, as it sheds light on the human dimension of a crisis that continues to impact countless lives. Through education and awareness, it is possible to foster a deeper understanding of the resilience and struggles of those who embark on these perilous journeys in search of a better future.

Modes of Transportation

Transportation has played a crucial role in the journey of Africans across the Mediterranean, especially during the transatlantic slave trade. The various modes of transportation used by individuals fleeing dire circumstances or seeking better opportunities significantly influenced their experiences. The primary methods included small boats, larger vessels, and sometimes overland routes that led to Mediterranean ports. Each mode of transportation carried its own risks and challenges, shaping the narrative of migration and the transition into slavery.

Small boats, often overcrowded and poorly equipped, were commonly used by those attempting to escape from coastal regions of Africa. These vessels, manned by local fishermen or smugglers, were typically made from wood and lacked adequate safety features. The journey across the Mediterranean in such small crafts was fraught with danger, including the threat of capsising, harsh weather conditions, and encounters with naval patrols. Many who undertook this perilous voyage faced dehydration, starvation, and the constant fear of being intercepted before reaching safety.

Larger ships, often operated by slave traders, represented a different mode of transportation that had a profound impact on the fate of many Africans. These vessels were designed to carry large numbers of captives, packed tightly into the hold under brutal conditions. The journey across the sea could take weeks, and during this time, individuals were subjected to unspeakable horrors, including disease, malnutrition, and violence. The conditions aboard these ships were inhumane, with little regard for the lives of those being transported. The experience of crossing the Mediterranean in such ships marked a significant transition from freedom to bondage.

In addition to maritime routes, some Africans undertook overland journeys to reach Mediterranean ports. These routes often involved traversing difficult terrains and navigating through hostile territories. Travelers faced numerous obstacles, including banditry, natural barriers, and extreme weather conditions. The overland trek was often undertaken by those fleeing conflict or pursuing opportunities to connect with maritime networks, demonstrating the lengths to which individuals would go to escape their circumstances. These journeys highlighted the resourcefulness and resilience of those seeking a better life.

The modes of transportation utilised during these journeys not only reflect the physical movement of individuals but also serve as a metaphor for the broader experience of migration and enslavement. Understanding these methods provides insight into the historical context of African migration across the Mediterranean and the complexities involved in the journey towards Europe. Each mode of transportation is a testament to the struggle for survival and the enduring spirit of those who faced unimaginable challenges in their quest for freedom.

The Risks and Dangers of the Journey

The journey across the Mediterranean Sea is fraught with numerous risks and dangers that threaten the lives of those attempting to escape dire circumstances in their home countries. Many individuals set out with hopes of finding safety, opportunity, and a better future in Europe, yet the perils they face along the way can often overshadow these aspirations. The sheer physical challenges of the journey are exacerbated by the treacherous nature of the seas, which can be unpredictable and violent. Overcrowded and unseaworthy vessels, often operated by smugglers with little regard for human life, increase the likelihood of capsising or sinking, leading to tragic losses at sea.

In addition to the inherent dangers of the Mediterranean itself, migrants encounter a multitude of social and political threats. Human trafficking networks prey on vulnerable individuals, luring them with false promises of safety and support. Once entangled in these networks, migrants can find themselves subjected to exploitation, violence, and even forced labor. The lack of legal protection for these individuals often leaves them vulnerable to abuse and intimidation from both traffickers and local authorities, further complicating their journey and diminishing their chances for safe passage.

Moreover, the conditions in refugee camps and makeshift shelters along the route can be dire. Many migrants experience overcrowded living situations, insufficient access to basic necessities such as food, water, and medical care. These conditions can lead to a host of health issues, both physical and mental, as individuals grapple with the trauma of their experiences. The psychological toll of the journey is significant, with many facing anxiety, depression, and post-traumatic stress disorder as they navigate the uncertainties and dangers of their circumstances.

The political climate surrounding migration in Europe adds another layer of risk. Many countries have adopted strict immigration policies that often lead to increased hostility towards migrants. This environment can result in violent encounters with law enforcement or anti-immigrant groups, further jeopardizing the safety and well-being of those seeking refuge. The fear of deportation or being denied entry can discourage individuals from seeking help or accessing critical resources, forcing them to remain in precarious situations.

Ultimately, the journey across the Mediterranean embodies a complex interplay of hope and despair. While many embark on this perilous path in search of a better life, the risks they face are a stark reminder of the dangers inherent in their pursuit of freedom and safety. Addressing these challenges requires a concerted effort from governments, humanitarian organisations, and communities to create safer pathways for migrants and to advocate for their rights and dignity in the face of adversity.

Stories of Survival and Resilience

Stories of survival and resilience are woven into the narratives of countless individuals who have undertaken the perilous journey across the Mediterranean. These stories serve as powerful reminders of the human spirit's capacity to endure, adapt, and overcome adversity. Many of these migrants come from regions afflicted by conflict, poverty, and political instability. Their motivations for embarking on such dangerous voyages are often rooted in a desperate search for safety, opportunity, and a better future for themselves and their families. Each story is a testament to the determination and hope that fuel their journeys, even in the face of overwhelming odds.

One of the most striking aspects of these journeys is the physical and emotional challenges faced by migrants. Many embark on overcrowded and unseaworthy vessels, risking their lives to traverse the tumultuous waters of the Mediterranean. Survivors recount harrowing experiences of capsising, dehydration, and loss of loved ones during their voyages. These narratives highlight the dire conditions that drive individuals to make such sacrifices. Despite the trauma, many emerge from these experiences with a newfound strength and resilience, often becoming advocates for change and awareness regarding the plight of migrants.

The role of community and solidarity is also a recurring theme in stories of survival. Migrants often rely on each other for support during their journeys, forming bonds that transcend cultural and national boundaries. These relationships can be critical for emotional and physical survival, as shared experiences foster a sense of belonging and mutual aid. In many cases, individuals who have successfully reached their destinations return to assist others, creating a cycle of support that underscores the importance of community in overcoming adversity.

Furthermore, the experiences of women and children are particularly poignant in these narratives. Women often face additional layers of vulnerability, including gender-based violence and exploitation. Yet, many demonstrate remarkable resilience, finding ways to navigate their circumstances and protect their families. Their stories often highlight the strength of maternal bonds and the lengths to which they will go to ensure the safety and well-being of their children. These accounts shed light on the unique challenges faced by women in the migration process, while also celebrating their fortitude and resourcefulness.

Ultimately, the stories of survival and resilience among Africans crossing the Mediterranean serve as crucial reminders of the complexities of migration. They invite us to confront the harsh realities faced by these individuals while also celebrating their incredible strength and determination. By sharing these narratives, we can foster greater empathy and understanding, challenging the stereotypes and misconceptions that often surround discussions of migration. These stories not only illuminate the struggles of those who seek a better life but also inspire action towards creating a more just and compassionate world for all.

The Role of Humanitarian Organisations

Humanitarian organizations play a crucial role in addressing the challenges faced by Africans crossing the Mediterranean in search of safety and a better life. These organisations are dedicated to providing immediate assistance to those who find themselves in perilous situations during their journey. They offer essential services such as medical care, food, water, shelter, and psychological support to migrants and refugees. The presence of these organisations is vital in mitigating the risks associated with the treacherous crossing, which often leads to tragic outcomes due to overcrowded boats, adverse weather conditions, and the threat of human traffickers.

In addition to immediate relief efforts, humanitarian organisations advocate for the rights of migrants and refugees. They work tirelessly to raise awareness about the plight of those crossing the Mediterranean, highlighting the need for policies that protect human rights and ensure safe passage. These organisations often engage with governments and international bodies to influence policies that can lead to more humane treatment of migrants. Their advocacy is crucial in fostering an environment where the dignity and rights of individuals seeking refuge are upheld.

Humanitarian organisations also play an educational role, providing information on the dangers of illegal migration and the realities of life in destination countries. Many migrants embark on their journeys with unrealistic expectations, often fueled by misinformation. By disseminating accurate information about the risks and the legal options available, these organisations help individuals make informed decisions. This educational outreach is vital in reducing the number of people who fall prey to human traffickers and those who exploit vulnerable migrants.

Moreover, the work of humanitarian organisations is often collaborative, involving partnerships with local communities, governments, and other stakeholders. These collaborations enhance the effectiveness of their programs and ensure that aid is delivered in a culturally sensitive manner. By engaging local communities, humanitarian organizations can tap into valuable knowledge and resources, fostering a sense of solidarity and shared responsibility in addressing the challenges faced by migrants. This collective approach strengthens the overall impact of their efforts and helps to build resilient communities.

Finally, the ongoing challenges faced by humanitarian organisations, including limited funding, political opposition, and operational hazards, highlight the need for sustained support from the global community. The complexities of migration require a multifaceted response that includes not only immediate humanitarian aid but also long-term solutions to the root causes of migration. By supporting the efforts of these organisations, society can contribute to a more compassionate and effective response to the plight of Africans crossing the Mediterranean. Their work is essential in ensuring that the journey does not end in tragedy, but rather leads to hope and opportunity for a better future.

Chapter 6: Arrival in Europe

The Reception of Migrants

As thousands of Africans embark on perilous journeys in search of safety and better opportunities, the response of host countries and communities greatly influences their experiences upon arrival. This reception is often marked by a mix of humanitarian response, political discourse, and societal attitudes that can either facilitate integration or exacerbate tensions.

Upon reaching European shores, migrants frequently encounter a range of reception facilities designed to provide immediate assistance. These facilities vary widely in quality, with some offering essential services such as food, medical care, and shelter, while others may lack adequate resources. The conditions within these facilities can significantly impact the physical and mental well-being of migrants, particularly those who have endured traumatic experiences during their journey. Understanding the nature of these reception centers is critical for recognisng the challenges faced by newcomers and the importance of ensuring humane treatment.

The legal framework surrounding the reception of migrants is another crucial aspect that shapes their experiences. European countries have adopted various policies and regulations regarding asylum seekers and migrants. Some nations prioritize swift processing of claims, while others implement stricter border controls and asylum procedures. This legal landscape can create disparities in the treatment of migrants, leading to confusion and insecurity among those seeking refuge. Additionally, the political climate in host countries often influences these policies, with fluctuating public sentiment impacting government decisions.

Societal attitudes toward migrants play a significant role in determining their reception within local communities. In some regions, there is a strong sense of solidarity and support for those fleeing conflict and hardship, leading to grassroots initiatives aimed at fostering integration. Conversely, negative perceptions fueled by misinformation and fear can lead to hostility and discrimination. Understanding these societal dynamics is essential for promoting empathy and encouraging constructive dialogue about migration, helping to bridge the gap between migrants and host communities.

Ultimately, the reception of migrants crossing the Mediterranean reflects broader societal values and priorities. It highlights the need for a coordinated response that balances humanitarian obligations with the realities of political and social contexts. By examining the experiences of African migrants upon arrival in Europe, it becomes clear that their journeys do not end at the water's edge; rather, they embark on a new chapter filled with hope, challenge, and the ongoing quest for belonging in an unfamiliar land.

Legal Challenges and Asylum Seeking

Legal challenges faced by asylum seekers from Africa attempting to cross the Mediterranean are multi-faceted and often overwhelming. The journey is fraught with peril, not only due to the treacherous waters but also because of the complex legal frameworks that govern asylum and immigration in Europe. Many African migrants embark on this journey fleeing violence, persecution, or dire economic conditions, only to encounter significant obstacles once they reach European shores. The legal systems in various countries respond differently to these individuals, creating a patchwork of rights and protections that can complicate their efforts to seek asylum.

In many European countries, the legal process for applying for asylum can be lengthy and arduous. Upon arrival, migrants must navigate a series of bureaucratic hurdles, including registration, interviews, and appeals. These processes are not only time-consuming but can also be intimidating, particularly for individuals who may not be familiar with the legal language or requirements. The lack of legal representation exacerbates the situation, leaving many asylum seekers vulnerable to misunderstandings and misapplications of the law. This complexity can deter individuals from pursuing their claims or lead to the rejection of valid applications.

Additionally, the policies of various European countries regarding asylum seekers can change rapidly and often reflect broader political climates. Some nations have adapted stricter measures, including detention of migrants and expedited deportation processes, which can undermine the legal rights of asylum seekers. These policies can create an environment of fear and uncertainty, further complicating the journey for those fleeing dangerous circumstances. As a result, many are left in limbo, facing the threat of being sent back to the very situations they sought to escape.

The EU's Dublin Regulation, which determines which member state is responsible for processing an asylum application, has also posed significant challenges. This regulation can lead to "asylum shopping," where migrants attempt to navigate through multiple countries in search of better prospects for their claims. However, it can also result in individuals being sent back to countries with less favorable asylum conditions, where they may struggle to receive adequate support or protection. This system often disproportionately affects those from Africa, who may already be at a disadvantage due to the lack of resources and support networks in these transit countries.

Ultimately, the legal challenges associated with asylum seeking for African migrants crossing the Mediterranean reveal a complex interplay of human rights, national policies, and international obligations. Addressing these challenges requires not only a reevaluation of existing legal frameworks but also a commitment to uphold the dignity and rights of all individuals seeking refuge. As the journey across the Mediterranean continues to be fraught with danger, understanding these legal obstacles is crucial for fostering a more humane and just approach to asylum in Europe.

Cultural Integration and Community Building

Cultural integration and community building are essential aspects of understanding the journey of Africans across the Mediterranean, particularly in the context of historical and contemporary migrations. This subchapter explores how these elements play a significant role in shaping the experiences of African migrants, who often face the dual challenge of preserving their cultural identities while navigating new social landscapes in Europe. The interactions between different cultures can lead to enriching exchanges, yet they can also present obstacles that necessitate community solidarity and resilience.

Historically, the Mediterranean has served as a crossroads where diverse cultures intersect. For many Africans fleeing conflict, poverty, or persecution, the journey across the sea represents not only a search for safety and opportunity but also an encounter with varied cultural frameworks. Understanding how these migrants integrate into European societies reveals a complex tapestry of adaptation and resistance. Many Africans bring with them rich traditions, languages, and customs, which can significantly contribute to the multicultural fabric of their new communities. This cultural exchange often fosters mutual understanding and respect, enhancing social cohesion.

Community building is vital for African migrants as they establish new lives in unfamiliar territories. Upon arrival, many individuals seek out networks that provide support, resources, and a sense of belonging. These networks often take the form of community organisations, cultural associations, or informal groups that help newcomers navigate the challenges of settlement. Such organisations not only assist with practical needs like housing and employment but also serve as platforms for cultural expression and advocacy. By facilitating connections among migrants and between migrants and local populations, these communities can mitigate feelings of isolation and promote integration.

However, the process of cultural integration is not without its challenges. Migrants often face discrimination and prejudice, which can hinder their ability to fully participate in society. These barriers can create divisions within communities, making it essential for both migrants and host societies to engage in dialogues that foster understanding and empathy. Educational initiatives and cultural events can play a crucial role in bridging gaps between different groups, allowing for shared experiences that highlight commonalities rather than differences. Such efforts can pave the way for more inclusive environments where diversity is celebrated.

In conclusion, cultural integration and community building are critical components of the African migration experience across the Mediterranean. By recognizing the importance of these elements, stakeholders can work towards creating supportive environments that honor the rich heritage of African migrants while promoting their successful integration into European societies. This holistic approach not only enriches local communities but also contributes to a broader understanding of the shared human experience, emphasising the interconnectedness of our global society.

Chapter 7: The Legacy of Migration

Impact on African Communities

The impact of the trans-Mediterranean migration on African communities is seen as, altering social, economic, and cultural landscapes across the continent. The journey, often perilous and fraught with danger, has led to significant demographic changes, as families are separated, and communities are left to grapple with the absence of their members. This demographic shift can result in a loss of human capital, as many of those who undertake the journey are young, able individuals, leaving behind a gap in the workforce and a potential decline in community vitality.

Economically, the migration of Africans across the Mediterranean has created both challenges and opportunities for communities. On one hand, remittances sent back home can provide a crucial lifeline for families, enabling them to invest in education, health care, and local businesses. However, this reliance on remittances can also lead to economic instability, as communities may become dependent on the income generated by those who have migrated. Additionally, when migrants face hardships or exploitative conditions in their destination countries, the financial support that once flowed back home can diminish, leading to increased poverty and economic uncertainty.

Culturally, the journey across the Mediterranean has led to the emergence of new identities and the blending of traditions. As migrants encounter diverse cultures and experiences, they often return with new perspectives that can enrich their home communities. However, this cultural exchange can also create tensions, as traditional values may clash with new ideas and practices brought back by returnees. The challenge for many African communities lies in finding a balance between honoring their heritage and embracing the changes brought about by migration.

The trauma experienced by those who face violence, exploitation, or even death during their journey can leave lasting scars. The stigma associated with migration can also affect the reintegration of returnees, who may struggle to find their place within their communities after enduring such harrowing experiences. This psychological toll can foster an environment of fear and mistrust, complicating community cohesion and resilience.

Lastly, the impact of migration on African communities is further compounded by external factors such as government policies and international relations. Policies aimed at curbing migration often result in increased boarder security and harsher conditions for those attempting to cross, which can exacerbate the vulnerabilities faced by migrants. Additionally, the narratives surrounding migration in media and political discourse can shape public perception, influencing how communities view both migrants and the phenomenon of migration itself. Understanding these dynamics is crucial for addressing the challenges and opportunities that arise from the ongoing journey of Africans across the Mediterranean.

The Influence on European Society

The trans-Mediterranean journey of Africans has significantly shaped European society throughout history. This influence can be traced back to the early encounters between Africa and Europe, where cultural, economic, and social exchanges began to take root. The movement of Africans across the Mediterranean was not merely a tale of forced migration and slavery; it also facilitated the transfer of knowledge, traditions, and innovations that contributed to the development of various European cultures. The interplay between these two regions has left an indelible mark on the continent and continues to resonate in contemporary European society.

The arrival of Africans in Europe often brought new agricultural practices and culinary influences. For instance, the introduction of African crops and farming techniques helped diversify European agriculture. The incorporation of ingredients such as sorghum and millet altered the European diet, introducing new flavors and nutritional options. Additionally, the fusion of African cooking methods with European culinary traditions laid the groundwork for an evolving gastronomic landscape that reflects the continent's multicultural heritage. These agricultural and culinary exchanges are a testament to how the African presence in Europe enriched local economies and societies.

Socially, the integration of Africans into European communities led to the emergence of hybrid cultural identities. As Africans settled in various regions, they contributed to the local arts, music, and religious practices. The blending of African and European artistic expressions gave rise to unique forms of music, dance, and visual art that are celebrated today. In cities where Africans were present, cultural festivals and events began to showcase the richness of this diversity, fostering a sense of unity and shared identity among different groups. This cultural exchange was crucial in shaping the social fabric of European communities, promoting tolerance and understanding.

In the early years, enslaved Africans were often forced to work in various sectors, from agriculture to domestic labour, which significantly contributed to the economic development of European nations. Their labour was integral to the growth of industries, particularly in the Mediterranean regions. Moreover, the wealth generated from the transatlantic slave trade and the exploitation of African labor fueled the expansion of European economies. This economic interdependence created a complex relationship between Africa and Europe, with lasting implications for both regions.

In contemporary times, the historical influence of Africans crossing the Mediterranean is reflected in ongoing discussions about migration, identity, and cultural exchange in Europe. As modern-day migrants continue to traverse these waters, the legacy of their ancestors shapes public perception and policy. The contributions of Africans to European society, whether through art, food, or labour, emphasise the importance of recognising and valuing multicultural heritage. Understanding this historical narrative is vital for fostering a more inclusive society that acknowledges the interconnectedness of cultures and promotes a shared future for all.

Ongoing Issues and Future Outlook

The ongoing issues surrounding the journey of Africans across the Mediterranean are deeply intertwined with historical, social, and economic factors. The legacy of colonialism continues to shape the experiences of many African migrants, as they face not only physical challenges in their journey but also systemic barriers upon arrival in Europe. The Mediterranean Sea, often referred to as a "graveyard" for migrants, highlights the perilous conditions they endure, including overcrowded boats, human trafficking, and exploitation. Despite international awareness, the European Union's policies often emphasise boarder control over humanitarian assistance, leaving many vulnerable individuals without adequate protection or support.

Human rights organisations have documented the increasing dangers faced by migrants attempting to cross the Mediterranean. Reports of pushbacks, where migrants are forcibly returned to unsafe conditions, have raised significant ethical concerns regarding the treatment of these individuals. Additionally, the rise of anti-immigrant sentiment in various European countries complicates the situation further. This hostile environment not only affects the immediate safety of migrants but also influences their long-term integration into society. As public opinion shifts, many migrants find themselves navigating an uncertain landscape fraught with legal challenges and societal rejection.

The economic factors driving migration remain a pressing issue as well. Many Africans embark on this treacherous journey in search of better opportunities to escape poverty, unemployment, and political instability. The impact of climate change also plays a significant role in exacerbating these challenges, with agricultural disruptions leading to food insecurity and displacement. Addressing these root causes requires comprehensive strategies that go beyond border management and encompass development aid, economic support, and capacity building in home countries. Only by tackling these issues can the cycle of migration driven by desperation be effectively mitigated.

Looking ahead, the future outlook for African migrants crossing the Mediterranean hinges on the evolution of policies and international cooperation. As the global community confronts the realities of migration, there is a growing recognition of the need for a more balanced approach that prioritizes human rights and safety. Collaborative efforts between African nations and European countries can facilitate better management of migration flows while ensuring that migrants are treated with dignity. Furthermore, fostering dialogue between governments, civil society, and migrants themselves can lead to more effective solutions that address both immediate needs and long-term integration goals.

In conclusion, the journey of Africans across the Mediterranean continues to be fraught with ongoing issues that require urgent attention. The interplay of historical legacies, economic pressures, and political dynamics shapes the experiences of those who undertake this perilous journey. As we move forward, it is crucial to focus on comprehensive policies that reflect a commitment to human rights, economic development, and international collaboration. Addressing these challenges is not just a humanitarian obligation; it is essential for fostering a more equitable and just global society.

Chapter 8: Personal Narratives

Testimonies from Migrants

Testimonies from migrants provide a profound understanding of the harrowing experiences faced by individuals embarking on perilous journeys across the Mediterranean. These narratives reveal the complex motivations behind migration, often rooted in dire economic conditions, political instability, and social unrest in their home countries. Through the voices of those who have navigated these treacherous waters, we gain insight into the sacrifices made in pursuit of a better life, as well as the harsh realities that often await them upon arrival.

Many migrants recount the moment they decided to leave their homeland, often marked by desperation and a lack of options. For some, the choice to embark on such a dangerous journey stem from the desire to escape violence or persecution. Others seek economic opportunities that are unattainable in their home countries. The testimonies illustrate a common theme: the hope for a brighter future drives individuals to risk everything, even their lives, in search of safety and prosperity.

The journey across the Mediterranean is fraught with danger, and migrants' accounts emphasise the physical and emotional toll of this experience. Many describe harrowing tales of overcrowded boats, treacherous weather, and the constant threat of drowning. The fear of being intercepted by authorities or falling prey to human traffickers adds another layer of anxiety to their journey. These stories highlight the resilience of the human spirit, as migrants confront unimaginable challenges in their quest for freedom.

Upon reaching Europe, the realities often differ significantly from the dreams that propelled them across the sea. Many migrants face discrimination, exploitation, and a lack of access to basic resources. The testimonies reveal that what they envisioned as a new beginning often turns into a struggle for survival in unfamiliar environments. The disillusionment can be profound, as they grapple with the gap between their aspirations and the harsh truths of their new lives.

Despite the challenges, the testimonies from migrants also reflect a sense of hope and determination. Many express gratitude for the support received from local communities and organisations that aid their integration. These narratives emphasise the importance of solidarity and compassion in addressing the plight of migrants. By sharing their stories, these individuals not only seek to raise awareness about the issues they face but also contribute to a broader conversation about migration, humanity, and the need for systemic change.

Stories of Success and Struggle

The Mediterranean Sea has long served as a bridge and a barrier for countless Africans seeking a better life. Among the stories of those who have crossed its waters, some resonate with triumph while others reveal profound struggles. The narratives of individuals and families fleeing conflict, poverty, and instability highlight the complexities of migration. Each story is unique, yet they collectively illustrate the harsh realities faced by many who embark on this perilous journey in search of hope and opportunity.

One compelling account comes from a young woman named Amina, who left her home in Eritrea. Facing conscription into a military regime and limited opportunities for women, Amina decided to risk everything for the chance at education and freedom. Her journey across the Mediterranean was fraught with danger, including the threat of human trafficking and the perils of overcrowded boats. Amina's resilience shines through as she navigated these challenges, ultimately reaching Italy, where she began to rebuild her life. Her story exemplifies the courage of many who dare to dream of a better future despite overwhelming obstacles.

In contrast, the story of Ibrahim, a father from Syria, illustrates the heart-wrenching choices families must make. After losing nearly everything to civil war, Ibrahim set out with his wife and two young children. The family faced treacherous conditions during their crossing, including encounters with smugglers who exploited their desperation. Tragically, during a tumultuous night at sea, Ibrahim lost his wife to the waves. His struggle to provide for his children while grappling with grief underscores the profound emotional toll that migration can take. Ibrahim's journey emphasizes the human cost of seeking safety and stability.

These narratives reflect broader themes of resilience and community. Many migrants find strength in solidarity, forming bonds with fellow travelers who share similar experiences. In camps and communities upon arrival in Europe, they often create networks of support, helping one another navigate the complexities of a new life. The stories of success are often built on this foundation of mutual aid, where individuals work together to overcome barriers, from learning a new language to securing employment. This communal effort highlights the importance of connection and solidarity in the face of adversity.

Ultimately, the tales of success and struggle among Africans crossing the Mediterranean serve as powerful reminders of the human spirit's endurance. They challenge us to look beyond statistics and policies, urging a deeper understanding of the motivations and experiences of migrants. As schools, libraries, colleges, and universities engage with these narratives, they have the opportunity to foster empathy and awareness, encouraging discussions about migration, identity, and resilience. Through storytelling, the journeys of Amina, Ibrahim, and countless others can inspire a more compassionate response to the complexities of migration in today's world.

The voices of families left behind

The migration of Africans across the Mediterranean often carries with it a heavy burden, not only for those who embark on the perilous journey but also for the families left behind. The voices of these families resonate with a mix of hope, despair, and resilience. They live in a state of uncertainty, grappling with the absence of their loved ones who seek a better life across the sea. The emotional and psychological impact experienced by families as they wait for news, often clinging to the hope that their loved ones will succeed in their journey.

Families left behind often face significant socio-economic challenges, exacerbated by the absence of key breadwinners. In many cases, the decision to migrate is made with the understanding that the potential for remittances can provide financial stability. However, when communication becomes sporadic or ceases altogether, families may find themselves in dire straits. The emotional toll of uncertainty can lead to increased anxiety and distress, as relatives grapple with feelings of abandonment and loss, even while holding onto the dreams of reunion and prosperity.

Moreover, the narratives of families are often shaped by the media coverage of migration crises, which can be both informative and misleading. While some stories highlight the dangers of the journey, others focus solely on the economic aspects, neglecting the personal experiences of those left behind. This portrayal can create a skewed perception in society, leading to a lack of understanding regarding the motivations behind migration. Families are not only defined by their economic status but also by their relationships, cultures, and the hopes they hold for a brighter future.

The emotional landscape of families can also lead to a sense of community among those who share similar experiences. In many communities, support networks form as families connect with others who have experienced similar losses or anxieties. These networks can provide a vital source of strength, allowing families to share resources, information, and emotional support. Such solidarity underscores the enduring bonds of kinship and the shared struggles of those navigating the complexities of migration.

Ultimately, the stories of families left behind are a crucial part of the broader narrative of migration across the Mediterranean. By amplifying their voices, we gain a deeper understanding of the human experience behind the statistics. These families embody resilience in the face of adversity, highlighting the emotional and social dimensions of migration that often remain in the shadows. Their experiences remind us that migration is not just a journey of individuals but a collective experience that reverberates through families and communities, shaping lives in profound ways.

Chapter 9: Advocacy and policy

Current Policies Affecting Migration

Current policies affecting migration across the Mediterranean are shaped by a complex interplay of national interests, European Union regulations, and international agreements. As African migrants undertake perilous journeys in search of better opportunities, the policies governing their movement play a critical role in determining their outcomes. Many countries have adapted restrictive measures aimed at curbing the influx of migrants, while others have implemented more humane approaches that acknowledge the need for protection and support. These policies often reflect broader geopolitical considerations, including trade agreements, security concerns, and diplomatic relations with countries of origin and transit.

The European Union has established a framework of policies that directly impact migration patterns. The Dublin Regulation, for instance, mandates that asylum seekers must apply for protection in the first EU country they enter, creating a burden on frontline states such as Italy and Greece. This policy has been criticised for leading to overcrowded reception centers and inadequate support for migrants. In response to the challenges posed by irregular migration, the EU has also invested in border control measures, including the establishment of Frontex, the European Boarder and Coast Guard Agency, which aims to enhance the security of external borders but has often been criticised for its role in human rights violations at sea.

Bilateral agreements between European nations and African countries have also shaped migration flows. These agreements often involve the transfer of funds or resources in exchange for cooperation in controlling migration. For instance, the partnership between Italy and Libya has resulted in the interception and return of thousands of migrants attempting to cross the Mediterranean. While proponents argue that these agreements help manage migration and prevent human trafficking, critics contend that they undermine the rights of migrants and expose them to dangerous conditions in detention centers.

In recent years, there has been a growing recognition of the need for comprehensive migration policies that address the root causes of migration. Initiatives aimed at fostering economic development, improving governance, and addressing conflicts in African countries are essential for creating conditions that reduce the need for individuals to embark on hazardous journeys. Organizations such as the International Organisation for Migration advocate for policies that support safe and legal migration pathways, emphasising the importance of addressing the socio-economic factors that drive migration.

As policies continue to evolve, it is crucial to consider the human impact of migration management strategies. The experiences of African migrants crossing the Mediterranean highlight the importance of creating a balanced approach that prioritises human rights while addressing security and economic concerns. Policymakers must engage with civil society, migrant communities, and international organisations to develop solutions that respect the dignity and rights of individuals seeking a better life. Only through inclusive dialogue and cooperation can effective policies be crafted to navigate the complexities of migration in a rapidly changing global landscape.

THE ROLE OF NGOS AND Activists

Non-governmental organizations (NGOs) and activists play a crucial role in addressing the complex issues surrounding the journeys of Africans crossing the Mediterranean. These organisations often act as a bridge between vulnerable migrants and the broader international community, raising awareness about the humanitarian crises faced by those fleeing conflict, poverty, or persecution in their home countries. By documenting the experiences of migrants and highlighting their struggles, NGOs help to humanise the statistics often presented in media reports, capturing the individual stories that reflect the broader systemic issues at play.

One of the primary functions of NGOs in this context is to provide direct assistance to migrants and refugees. Many NGOs operate rescue missions in the Mediterranean Sea, conducting search-and-rescue operations to save those at risk of drowning. These efforts are often met with challenges, including legal restrictions and hostile political environments, yet organisations such as Médecins Sans Frontières (Doctors Without Borders) and Sea-Watch continue to advocate for the rights of migrants while providing medical care and essential supplies. Their work underscores the urgent need for humanitarian intervention in situations where national governments may fail to protect vulnerable populations.

Activists associated with these NGOs also engage in advocacy and policy reform, challenging governmental policies that contribute to the suffering of migrants. This includes lobbying for safer migration routes, the right to asylum, and improving conditions in detention centers. Through campaigns, protests, and public speaking, activists aim to influence public opinion and encourage governments to adopt more humane policies. They often collaborate with international bodies, such as the United Nations, to create frameworks that prioritise human rights and dignity for all individuals, regardless of their migration status.

Furthermore, NGOs and activists play a significant role in raising awareness about the root causes of migration. By conducting research and disseminating information, they shed light on issues such as economic inequality, political instability, and climate change, which compel individuals to leave their homes. Understanding these underlying factors is essential for developing comprehensive solutions that address not only the symptoms of migration but also its causes. Educational programs and community outreach initiatives help to inform the public about these complex dynamics, fostering a more empathetic approach to migration and its associated challenges.

In conclusion, the contributions of NGOs and activists are indispensable in the fight for the rights of Africans crossing the Mediterranean. Their tireless efforts to provide direct support, advocate for policy change, and raise awareness about the root causes of migration are essential in shaping a more just and humane response to this global crisis. As the journeys across the Mediterranean continue to be fraught with danger, the work of these organisations serves as a reminder of the resilience of the human spirit and the collective responsibility to protect those in need.

RECOMMENDATIONS FOR Change

The journey of Africans across the Mediterranean has been fraught with peril and laden with historical significance. To foster a more comprehensive understanding of this migration, educational institutions such as schools, libraries, colleges, and universities should consider implementing curriculum changes that emphasise the historical context, the individual stories of migrants, and the socio-economic factors driving this exodus. Integrating these elements into existing programs can provide students and community members with a nuanced view of the complexities surrounding this issue.

One recommendation is to develop interdisciplinary courses that explore the historical, political, and economic dimensions of African migration to Europe. These courses could include perspectives from history, sociology, political science, and economics to provide a well-rounded understanding. This approach encourages critical thinking and fosters a deeper empathy for those involved in such harrowing journeys.

Additionally, libraries and educational institutions should curate collections that highlight literature and research related to African migration across the Mediterranean. This can include personal narratives, academic studies, and historical accounts that shed light on the human experience behind the statistics. Hosting events such as author talks, documentary screenings, and panel discussions can further enrich the community's understanding. These activities not only promote awareness but also create a platform for dialogue about the ongoing challenges faced by migrants today.

Furthermore, partnerships with local organizations and NGOs that work with migrants can enhance the educational experience. By facilitating internships, volunteer opportunities, and collaborative projects, students can gain firsthand insights into the lives of migrants and the systemic issues they confront. This engagement fosters a sense of responsibility and activism among students, equipping them with the tools to advocate for social justice and policy reform in their communities.

Finally, it is crucial to incorporate technology and digital storytelling into educational initiatives surrounding this topic. Utilizing social media platforms, podcasts, and online forums can help amplify the voices of migrants and share their stories with a broader audience. By harnessing the power of technology, educational institutions can create dynamic and interactive learning environments that resonate with younger generations. This approach not only raises awareness but also inspires action, encouraging students to become informed and engaged citizens in a globalised world.

Chapter 10: Conclusion

R eflections on the Journey
    The journey of Africans across the Mediterranean is steeped in a complex history that intertwines themes of survival, resilience, and the quest for dignity. As we reflect on this journey, motivations that drive individuals to embark on such perilous paths. Many are fleeing conflict, persecution, and economic hardship in their home countries. This migration often represents the desperate search for a better life, a pursuit of opportunities that seem unattainable within the confines of their native lands. Understanding these motivations allows us to grasp the broader context of this migration and the human spirit's determination to seek safety and prosperity.

The Mediterranean crossing has become synonymous with tragedy, as countless lives have been lost in the attempt to reach European shores. The perilous nature of this journey is marked by overcrowded boats, inadequate supplies, and the ever-present threat of exploitation. Survivors often recount harrowing tales of desperation and loss. These stories serve as poignant reminders of the human cost associated with migration and the urgency of addressing the systemic issues that contribute to such hazardous journeys. While the focus is frequently placed on the statistics of migration, it is essential to remember the individuals behind these numbers, each with unique stories and aspirations.

The role of international policies and responses to this migration crisis also warrants reflection. Governments and organisations grapple with the challenges of managing migration while ensuring the protection of human rights. The responses have ranged from stringent border controls to humanitarian efforts aimed at providing aid and support to those in transit. However, these measures often reflect a tension between national security concerns and the moral imperative to protect vulnerable populations. A critical examination of these policies is necessary to foster a more compassionate and effective approach to migration that prioritizes human dignity and safety.

The narratives surrounding African migration to Europe often lack nuance, perpetuating stereotypes and misconceptions. Media portrayals can sometimes dehumanise migrants, reducing them to mere statistics or threats rather than recognising their humanity and agency. It is essential for educational institutions to engage with these narratives critically, promoting a more informed and empathetic understanding of the complexities involved. By amplifying the voices of migrants and sharing their experiences, we can challenge dominant narratives and foster a more inclusive discourse on migration.

In conclusion, reflecting on the journey of Africans across the Mediterranean encourages us to confront the realities of migration, recognising both the challenges and the resilience of those who undertake this journey. It calls for a collective responsibility to advocate for policies that uphold human rights and dignity while addressing the root causes of migration. Through education, awareness, and compassion, we can foster a deeper understanding of the journeys undertaken by individuals seeking a better future, ultimately contributing to a more just and equitable world for all.

The Importance of Understanding Migration

Understanding migration, particularly the movement of Africans across the Mediterranean, is crucial for grasping the complexities of contemporary global dynamics. This phenomenon is not merely a statistical occurrence; it embodies the stories, struggles, and aspirations of millions seeking better lives. Historical contexts, socio-economic drivers, and geopolitical factors all converge to illuminate why individuals embark on perilous journeys across treacherous waters. Grasping these elements fosters a deeper comprehension of migration's implications, both for the migrants and the societies they leave and enter.

The Mediterranean Sea, often referred to as a gateway, has become synonymous with the plight of African migrants seeking refuge and opportunities in Europe. The reasons for this migration are manifold, ranging from armed conflict and political instability to poverty and environmental degradation. Understanding these motivations is vital for addressing the root causes of migration rather than merely responding to its effects. This perspective encourages a more empathetic approach, recognizing that migrants are not just statistics but individuals with unique stories and aspirations shaped by their circumstances.

Furthermore, understanding migration reveals the interconnectedness of global issues, such as human rights, economic disparity, and climate change. The journeys undertaken by many migrants are fraught with danger, and their experiences often culminate in exploitation and human trafficking. By educating communities on these harsh realities, we foster a sense of responsibility and advocacy for policies that protect vulnerable populations. Awareness of these challenges can also inspire initiatives that promote safer migration pathways and greater collaboration among countries to address the underlying issues of forced migration.

In educational settings, discussing migration helps cultivate critical thinking and empathy among students. By exploring the historical and contemporary factors that drive migration, learners can engage with the complexities of human mobility and its impact on global society. This dialogue not only enriches their understanding of current events but also encourages them to consider solutions that promote justice and dignity for all individuals, regardless of their origin. Schools and universities play a pivotal role in shaping informed citizens who can contribute positively to discussions surrounding migration and human rights.

Ultimately, understanding migration is essential for fostering a more inclusive and compassionate world. The stories of Africans crossing the Mediterranean are not just tales of desperation; they are narratives of resilience and hope. By illuminating these experiences, we encourage a broader recognition of our shared humanity. As we engage with these topics in libraries, schools, and universities, we contribute to a culture of awareness and action that emphasises the importance of solidarity and support for those navigating the challenges of migration.

Looking Towards a More Inclusive Future

Looking towards a more inclusive future necessitates a holistic understanding of the historical and contemporary challenges faced by Africans attempting to cross the Mediterranean. The journey across this perilous body of water has been fraught with danger and desperation, often leading to tragic outcomes. However, acknowledging these narratives is vital for fostering empathy and awareness among younger generations in educational settings. By integrating the stories of these individuals into curricula, schools and universities can cultivate a sense of responsibility and action among students, encouraging them to advocate for social justice and equality.

Education plays a pivotal role in shaping perceptions about migration and the experiences of those who undertake such journeys. By providing comprehensive resources about the complexities of migration, educators can dispel myths and foster a more nuanced understanding of the socio-economic and political factors driving people to leave their homes. This includes discussions about poverty, conflict, and the search for better opportunities. Incorporating diverse perspectives, particularly those of migrants themselves, can enrich classroom discussions and promote critical thinking about global citizenship and human rights.

Furthermore, building partnerships between educational institutions and organisations dedicated to advocating for migrants' rights can amplify the voices of those who have crossed the Mediterranean. Collaborative projects, guest lectures, and community outreach initiatives can bridge the gap between academic knowledge and real-world experiences. This not only enhances students' learning but also instills a sense of agency, motivating them to become advocates for change. By engaging with organisations that work directly with migrants, students can gain firsthand insights into the challenges and triumphs of these journeys.

In fostering an inclusive future, it is essential to address systemic inequalities that perpetuate the marginalization of migrants. Educational institutions can lead by example, implementing policies that promote diversity and inclusion within their own communities. This includes providing support for students from migrant backgrounds and ensuring that their stories are represented in school narratives. By creating an environment where all students feel valued and heard, schools can play a transformative role in challenging prejudice and fostering a culture of understanding and respect.

Ultimately, looking towards a more inclusive future requires a commitment to continual learning and engagement with the complexities of migration. As institutions of learning, schools, libraries, colleges, and universities have the unique opportunity to shape the perspectives of future generations. By prioritising the inclusion of African migration narratives and fostering an environment of empathy and advocacy, these institutions can contribute to a more equitable society where the journeys of those crossing the Mediterranean are recognized not as mere statistics, but as vital human stories that demand our attention and action.

Chapter 11: Understanding the Refugee Crisis

Another significant aspect to consider is the demographic profile of refugees. A considerable proportion of those fleeing their countries are women and children, who often face heightened risks of violence, exploitation, and discrimination. Statistics indicate that over half of the world's refugees are under the age of 18. This demographic shift necessitates targeted interventions that not only provide immediate relief but also focus on education, health, and psychosocial support for young refugees and their families. Empowering these vulnerable groups is vital for fostering resilience and enabling them to contribute to their communities.

MOREOVER, RECENT DATA reveals a growing trend of climate-induced displacement, which is becoming a critical factor in the refugee crisis. Environmental degradation, extreme weather events, and resource scarcity are driving people from their homes, particularly in regions already affected by conflict. The International Organization for Migration (IOM) estimates that by 2050, climate change could displace over 200 million people globally. Recognizing the interplay between climate change and migration is essential for developing comprehensive policies that address both issues simultaneously and support affected populations in adapting to their changing environments.

Finally, as the global refugee crisis continues to evolve, international cooperation and solidarity are paramount. Many host countries, especially in the Global South, are facing immense pressure to accommodate large numbers of refugees with limited resources. Support from wealthier nations, both in terms of financial assistance and the sharing of responsibility, is crucial for alleviating the burden on host communities. By investing in sustainable development initiatives and enhancing local capacities, the international community can help create conditions that allow refugees to thrive in their own countries, ultimately reducing the need for dangerous migrations across borders.

Mediterranean Crossing
Humanitarian Response at Sea

Humanitarian response at sea has emerged as a critical aspect of addressing the multifaceted challenges faced by refugees attempting to cross the Mediterranean in search of safety and stability. The Mediterranean Sea, often referred to as a graveyard for those fleeing conflict and persecution, has become a focal point for humanitarian organizations striving to save lives and provide assistance. These organizations operate under the premise that immediate action is necessary to prevent loss of life and to uphold human dignity. Their efforts encompass search and rescue operations, medical assistance, and the provision of essential supplies to those intercepted at sea.

The complexities of humanitarian response at sea are compounded by the political and legal frameworks governing maritime activities. International laws, including the United Nations Convention on the Law of the Sea, dictate that vessels in distress must be provided with assistance. However, the enforcement of these laws can be inconsistent, often influenced by national policies and regional agreements. As a result, humanitarian organizations frequently find themselves navigating a treacherous landscape of competing interests, where the need for human rights protection clashes with national security concerns. It is vital for the public to understand these dynamics, as they directly impact the lives of vulnerable populations.

In addition to immediate rescue efforts, humanitarian responses at sea also include advocacy for the rights of refugees and displaced persons. Organizations work to raise awareness about the plight of those fleeing their homelands, highlighting the systemic issues that force individuals to embark on perilous journeys. By amplifying the voices of refugees and sharing their stories, these organizations aim to foster a more informed public discourse on migration and displacement. This advocacy is essential in shifting perceptions and encouraging policies that prioritize humanitarian needs over restrictive border controls.

Moreover, the role of local communities and governments in humanitarian response cannot be overlooked. Cooperation between humanitarian organizations and host countries is crucial for creating effective strategies to manage the influx of refugees. Local actors can provide invaluable insights and resources, fostering a collaborative environment that enhances the overall response. Engaging with communities not only strengthens the immediate humanitarian efforts but also promotes long-term solutions that address the root causes of displacement, ultimately enabling refugees to remain in their home countries whenever possible.

In conclusion, the humanitarian response at sea is an essential component of addressing the refugee crisis, particularly in the context of the Mediterranean crossings. It requires a comprehensive understanding of legal, political, and social dimensions to be effective. By highlighting the urgency of the situation and advocating for the rights of refugees, we can work towards a more humane approach to migration. Engaging the public in these discussions is vital, as collective awareness and action can lead to more effective solutions that not only save lives at sea but also support efforts to improve conditions for refugees in their countries of origin.

Chapter 12: Root Causes of Displacement

War and Conflict

War and conflict have been pivotal drivers of displacement, forcing millions to flee their homelands in search of safety and stability. The ongoing conflicts in regions such as the Middle East and North Africa have created a dynamic crisis, significantly impacting countries bordering the Mediterranean Sea. Understanding the root causes of these conflicts is essential to addressing refugee situations effectively. Factors such as political instability, ethnic tensions, and economic disparities contribute to the rise of violence, which not only disrupts the lives of individuals but also destabilizes entire communities and nations.

The impact of war extends beyond the immediate loss of life and property; it creates an environment of fear and uncertainty that drives families to seek refuge elsewhere. In many cases, the journey to Europe becomes a perilous path marked by treacherous crossings and exploitation. Refugees often face harrowing experiences at sea, where overcrowded boats, inadequate supplies, and the threat of drowning are constant dangers. The Mediterranean has become a graveyard for many, highlighting the desperate circumstances that compel people to undertake such risks. By examining these challenges, we can better understand the urgency of providing support within their countries of origin.

Efforts to address the refugee crisis must extend beyond immediate humanitarian assistance. To support refugees in their homelands, it is crucial to focus on conflict resolution and peacebuilding initiatives. Engaging local communities and fostering dialogue among conflicting parties can help to create sustainable solutions that reduce violence and promote stability. International organizations, governments, and civil society must work collaboratively to establish programs that address the underlying issues of conflict, including governance, social cohesion, and economic opportunities. Investing in these areas can help to mitigate the factors that drive people from their homes.

Education plays a vital role in this process, offering a pathway to empowerment and resilience. When individuals, especially youth, are provided with access to quality education, they are better equipped to contribute to their communities and shape their futures. Educational initiatives can help build critical thinking and conflict resolution skills, enabling communities to address grievances without resorting to violence. Furthermore, education can raise awareness of rights and opportunities available within their own countries, thereby reducing the allure of migration to uncertain futures abroad.

Ultimately, the goal of supporting refugees in their homelands lies in fostering an environment where people feel safe and valued. By addressing the root causes of war and conflict, and by empowering individuals through education and community engagement, we can create conditions that allow people to thrive in their own countries. This approach not only helps to alleviate the refugee crisis but also strengthens the fabric of society, benefiting both the individuals and the nations they inhabit. The challenge is significant, but with a concerted effort from the international community, it is possible to create a more stable and secure future for those affected by conflict.

Economic Instability

Economic instability is a significant factor contributing to the migration of refugees, particularly from regions affected by conflict, political unrest, and environmental challenges. In many cases, these economic hardships are compounded by a lack of opportunities, inadequate infrastructure, and the disruption of social services. This instability not only drives individuals to seek better prospects abroad but also undermines the potential for communities to rebuild and thrive in their homelands. Understanding the root causes of this instability is crucial for developing effective strategies that can support refugees and enable them to remain in their countries.

One of the primary drivers of economic instability in many regions is conflict. Wars and prolonged violence create an environment where businesses cannot operate, employment opportunities dwindle, and basic services become scarce. As individuals flee their homes to escape violence, they often leave behind their livelihoods, exacerbating the cycle of poverty. Moreover, the economic fallout from conflict can persist long after the fighting has ceased, as communities struggle to recover in the absence of investment and infrastructure. Addressing these issues requires concerted efforts to promote peace and stability, enabling populations to rebuild their economies and lives without the need to migrate.

Another critical aspect of economic instability is the impact of climate change, which disproportionately affects vulnerable populations in developing countries. Droughts, floods, and other extreme weather events can devastate agricultural production, leading to food insecurity and loss of income. These environmental challenges often force families to abandon their homes in search of more favorable conditions. Supporting sustainable practices and investing in climate resilience can help mitigate these impacts, allowing communities to adapt and thrive despite the challenges posed by a changing environment. By enhancing local capacities, we can create a more stable economic foundation that reduces the impetus for migration.

Additionally, systemic issues such as corruption and lack of governance play a crucial role in perpetuating economic instability. In many regions, weak institutions fail to provide the necessary support for economic development, resulting in inequality and limited access to resources. This environment fuels despair and drives individuals to seek opportunities elsewhere. Strengthening governance, promoting transparency, and fostering inclusive economic policies are essential steps toward creating a more equitable society. By addressing these systemic barriers, we can empower individuals to invest in their communities and contribute to sustainable development.

Finally, the role of international support and cooperation cannot be overlooked in addressing economic instability. Global partnerships can provide critical resources for rebuilding and development, enabling countries to implement effective economic policies and social programs. Encouraging investment in local economies and ensuring that aid reaches those who need it most are vital strategies in this regard. By fostering a collaborative approach that prioritizes the needs of vulnerable populations, we can create a more stable economic environment that allows refugees to remain in their homelands and rebuild their lives with dignity and hope.

Environmental Factors

Environmental factors play a crucial role in shaping the conditions that lead individuals to seek refuge in other countries. Climate change, natural disasters, and environmental degradation are increasingly recognized as significant contributors to forced migration. In many regions, particularly those that are already vulnerable, the impact of environmental changes can exacerbate existing socio-economic challenges, pushing communities to the brink. Understanding these environmental factors is essential for developing effective interventions aimed at supporting refugees in their homelands and preventing their perilous journeys across the Mediterranean Sea.

Climate change is one of the most pressing environmental issues affecting the livelihoods of millions. Rising temperatures, altered precipitation patterns, and increased frequency of extreme weather events can lead to crop failures, water scarcity, and loss of arable land. In countries where agriculture is the backbone of the economy, such changes can have devastating effects, leading to food insecurity and economic instability. Addressing the impacts of climate change through sustainable agricultural practices, improved water management, and investment in renewable energy sources can help communities build resilience and reduce the likelihood of forced migration.

Natural disasters, such as earthquakes, floods, and hurricanes, can also drive people from their homes. These events often result in immediate displacement, loss of property, and destruction of infrastructure. In many cases, communities are unable to recover fully from such disasters, leading to prolonged periods of instability. Supporting disaster preparedness and response initiatives is vital for mitigating the impact of these events. By investing in early warning systems, infrastructure improvements, and community training, organizations can help communities withstand and recover from natural disasters, ultimately reducing the need for individuals to seek refuge elsewhere.

Environmental degradation, including deforestation, pollution, and loss of biodiversity, further compounds the challenges faced by vulnerable communities. As natural resources become scarce, competition for these resources can lead to conflict and social unrest. It is essential to address the root causes of environmental degradation through sustainable development practices. Initiatives that promote conservation, sustainable land use, and community engagement can help protect the environment while fostering economic opportunities. By ensuring that communities have access to clean water, healthy ecosystems, and sustainable livelihoods, we can reduce the pressures that drive migration.

In conclusion, environmental factors are integral to understanding the complexities of forced migration. By recognizing the interplay between environmental challenges and socio-economic conditions, we can develop comprehensive strategies to support refugees in their homelands. This involves not only addressing immediate needs but also investing in long-term solutions that promote sustainability and resilience. Collaborative efforts among governments, NGOs, and local communities are essential to create an environment where individuals can thrive in their own countries, ultimately reducing the need for perilous journeys across borders.

Chapter 13: The Role of Host Countries

Legal Frameworks and Policies
Legal frameworks and policies play a crucial role in shaping the landscape of refugee support and protection, particularly for those seeking safety from conflict and persecution. International law, notably the 1951 Refugee Convention and its 1967 Protocol, outlines the rights of refugees and the obligations of states to protect them. These documents serve as foundational pillars for countries to develop their own legal systems regarding asylum seekers and refugees. While these international agreements provide a broad framework, individual nations often tailor their policies to reflect their social, political, and economic contexts, leading to significant variations in how refugees are treated worldwide.

Regional agreements also contribute to the legal landscape surrounding refugees. The European Union, for instance, has implemented measures such as the Dublin Regulation, which allocates responsibility for processing asylum applications among member states. This policy aims to prevent "asylum shopping," where individuals apply for asylum in multiple countries. However, this framework has faced criticism for placing disproportionate burdens on frontline states like Italy and Greece, raising questions about equity and the effectiveness of the collective responsibility model. The evolving nature of these regional policies highlights the need for a cohesive approach that balances national interests with humanitarian obligations.

In addition to international and regional frameworks, national laws dictate how refugees are treated upon arrival. Some countries adopt inclusive policies that facilitate integration through access to education, healthcare, and employment, while others implement restrictive measures that hinder refugees' chances of rebuilding their lives. Legal frameworks may also include provisions for temporary protection or resettlement opportunities, which can significantly impact refugees' prospects. Understanding these national policies is essential for advocates and organizations working to support refugees in their homelands, as they directly influence the resources and support available to displaced individuals.

Moreover, legal frameworks are not static; they are subject to change in response to political pressures, public opinion, and humanitarian crises. The rise of populism and anti-immigrant sentiment in various regions has led some countries to tighten their asylum policies, complicating efforts to provide support to refugees. Conversely, in times of humanitarian need, there may be movements toward more compassionate policies. Engaging with policymakers to advocate for robust legal protections and humane treatment of refugees is vital for ensuring that legal frameworks evolve to meet the changing needs of displaced populations.

Finally, the intersection of legal frameworks and policies with the broader socio-economic context cannot be overlooked. Effective refugee support is not solely a matter of legal compliance; it requires a comprehensive understanding of how laws are implemented on the ground. Collaboration between governments, NGOs, and local communities can help bridge gaps in legal protections and ensure that refugees receive the assistance they need. By fostering partnerships that promote legal awareness and support systems, stakeholders can work together to create an environment where refugees can thrive in their own countries, reducing the pressures that lead to dangerous journeys across borders.

Integration Challenges and Opportunities

The integration of refugees into their host communities presents both challenges and opportunities, particularly within the context of those crossing the Mediterranean Sea to Europe. Most refugees embark on perilous journeys fueled by the hope of a better life, often leaving behind their homes due to conflict, persecution, or economic hardship. However, while some may find refuge in new countries, the broader question remains: how can we support them in rebuilding their lives in their homelands? Addressing this issue requires a comprehensive understanding of the integration process and the multifaceted barriers that refugees face.

One of the primary challenges to integration is the socio-economic disparity between refugees and their host communities. Many refugees arrive with limited resources and face numerous obstacles in accessing employment, education, and healthcare. Consequently, they may struggle to establish a stable livelihood, which can lead to frustration and marginalization. Addressing these disparities requires targeted policies that not only facilitate access to essential services but also promote economic opportunities for refugees, allowing them to contribute meaningfully to their communities.

Cultural integration is another significant challenge. Refugees may encounter language barriers, social isolation, and cultural differences that hinder their ability to connect with locals. These factors can exacerbate feelings of alienation and anxiety, making it difficult for refugees to fully participate in society. To mitigate these challenges, initiatives that promote cultural exchange and community engagement can play a vital role. By fostering dialogue and understanding between refugees and host communities, we can build bridges that facilitate integration and mutual acceptance.

Despite these challenges, there are numerous opportunities for enhancing the integration of refugees. One promising approach is the promotion of local partnerships between governments, non-governmental organizations, and community groups. These collaborations can leverage resources and expertise to develop tailored solutions that address the specific needs of refugees. Moreover, by involving refugees in the decision-making process, we can empower them to take an active role in their integration, fostering a sense of ownership and belonging within their new communities.

Ultimately, the integration of refugees is not merely a challenge to be overcome but an opportunity for enriching host societies. By recognizing the strengths and contributions that refugees bring, we can create inclusive communities that benefit everyone. Supporting initiatives aimed at facilitating integration and addressing the root causes of displacement can lead to more sustainable solutions, enabling refugees to thrive in their homelands and reducing the need for treacherous journeys across the Mediterranean. Through collective action and commitment, we can transform the narrative surrounding refugees from one of challenge to one of opportunity and resilience.

The Impact on Local Communities

The arrival of refugees in a host country often brings significant changes to local communities, both positive and negative. Understanding these impacts is essential for fostering a supportive environment for refugees and ensuring the well-being of local populations. The integration of refugees can lead to economic revitalisation, as newcomers often bring diverse skills, entrepreneurial spirit, and a willingness to work. This influx can stimulate job creation and contribute to local economies, particularly in areas facing population decline or economic stagnation. Communities that embrace refugees may also experience cultural enrichment, benefiting from the introduction of new perspectives, traditions, and cuisines.

However, the integration of refugees also poses challenges to local communities. Competition for resources, such as housing, education, and healthcare, can create tension between established residents and newcomers. In some cases, local infrastructures may be strained, leading to perceptions of scarcity and resentment. This underlines the importance of proactive measures by governments and organisations to ensure that both refugees and local residents have access to essential services. Initiatives that promote shared resources and collaborative projects can help mitigate potential friction and foster a sense of unity.

Moreover, the impact of refugee influxes can vary significantly based on the community's prior experience with immigration. Communities that have previously welcomed newcomers may be better equipped to integrate refugees successfully, while those with little experience may struggle with the dynamics of cultural integration. Education and awareness campaigns can play a crucial role in preparing communities for the arrival of refugees. By fostering understanding and empathy, these initiatives can help to dispel myths and reduce xenophobia, paving the way for smoother transitions and mutual support.

Local governments and organizations play a key role in facilitating the integration process. Effective policies that encourage participation in community activities can help refugees feel more connected and valued. Programs that involve refugees in volunteer opportunities, local governance, or community decision-making can empower them and promote a sense of belonging. When refugees are seen as active contributors rather than burdens, it fosters a positive perception and strengthens community ties.

In conclusion, the impact of refugees on local communities is multifaceted, encompassing both challenges and opportunities. By recognising the potential benefits and addressing the concerns that may arise, communities can create an environment where both refugees and locals thrive. Supportive policies, community engagement, and education are essential components in this journey, ultimately leading to enriched and resilient communities that transcend borders and embrace diversity.

Chapter14: Supporting Refugees in Their Homelands
Development Aid and Economic Support

Development aid and economic support play crucial roles in addressing the root causes of forced migration, particularly for those seeking refuge in Europe from conflict-ridden regions. By investing in the economic stability and infrastructure of refugees' home countries, we can create environments where individuals are less inclined to leave their homes in search of safety and opportunity. This approach not only alleviates the pressure on European nations to accommodate rising numbers of asylum seekers but also fosters sustainable development in the regions most affected by displacement.

One of the primary ways development aid can support economic growth is through the enhancement of local governance and institutional capacities. Strong governance ensures that resources are effectively managed and distributed, leading to improved public services, infrastructure, and economic opportunities. By providing financial assistance and expertise to local governments, international aid organizations can help build resilient systems that support community development and empower citizens. This, in turn, reduces the likelihood of conflict and instability, which are often the driving forces behind migration.

Moreover, targeted investments in education and skill development are essential in creating a future where individuals feel they can thrive in their homeland. By equipping young people with the necessary skills and knowledge, development aid can help to reduce unemployment and underemployment, which are significant factors contributing to migration. Educational initiatives can also promote social cohesion and foster a sense of belonging, further encouraging individuals to remain in their communities and contribute to their local economies.

Economic support can also be directed toward fostering entrepreneurship and small business development. By providing microloans, training programs, and access to markets, aid organizations can empower local populations to generate their own income and create job opportunities. This not only bolsters the local economy but also instills a sense of agency and hope among individuals who may otherwise consider fleeing their homeland. Successful local enterprises can lead to a more stable economy, reducing the motivations that drive people to leave in search of better prospects abroad.

Finally, it is essential to recognize that development aid and economic support should be part of a comprehensive approach to addressing the challenges faced by refugees and their communities. Collaboration between governments, non-governmental organizations, and local stakeholders is vital to ensure that aid is effectively targeted and that the needs of the population are met. By fostering partnerships and encouraging local ownership of development initiatives, we can create lasting change that not only benefits refugees but also strengthens the fabric of their home countries, ultimately contributing to a more stable and prosperous world.

Education and Capacity Building

Education and capacity building play a crucial role in supporting refugees in their homelands, enabling them to develop the skills and opportunities necessary to thrive in their local communities. By investing in education, we can address the root causes of forced migration, empowering individuals and families to build sustainable futures without the need to undertake perilous journeys across the Mediterranean. This subchapter will explore various educational initiatives and capacity-building strategies that can effectively support refugees in their own countries.

One of the most effective ways to support education in refugee-affected regions is through the establishment of accessible learning centers. These centers can provide formal education, vocational training, and life skills programs tailored to the specific needs of displaced populations. By focusing on inclusive education that accommodates diverse learning styles and backgrounds, these centers can help refugees gain essential skills that are relevant to their local job markets. This approach not only improves individual prospects but also contributes to community resilience and economic stability.

In addition to formal education, mentorship programs can significantly enhance the capacity of refugees to navigate their challenges. By pairing refugees with mentors from their communities or abroad, individuals can receive guidance in areas such as career planning, entrepreneurship, and personal development. Mentorship fosters a sense of belonging and support, helping refugees to build networks and access resources that may otherwise be out of reach. This connection to a broader community can be instrumental in increasing self-efficacy and motivation among refugees, encouraging them to pursue their goals.

Collaboration between local governments, international organizations, and NGOs is essential for creating sustainable educational frameworks. These partnerships can facilitate the sharing of resources, knowledge, and best practices, ensuring that educational initiatives are culturally sensitive and contextually relevant. Furthermore, by fostering a sense of ownership among local stakeholders, these collaborations can lead to more effective and sustainable capacity-building efforts. Engaging refugees in the design and implementation of educational programs ensures that their voices are heard and their needs are prioritized.

Finally, leveraging technology can play a transformative role in enhancing educational access for refugees. Digital platforms can provide online learning resources, virtual classrooms, and access to information that may not be available locally. By integrating technology into education and capacity-building initiatives, we can overcome geographical barriers and create more inclusive learning environments. This approach also prepares refugees for a digital economy, equipping them with the skills necessary to succeed in an increasingly interconnected world.

In conclusion, education and capacity building are critical components of supporting refugees in their homelands. By creating accessible learning opportunities, fostering mentorship, promoting collaboration, and leveraging technology, we can empower refugees to build better futures for themselves and their communities. Addressing the educational needs of refugees not only benefits individuals but also contributes to the overall stability and development of their home countries, reducing the pressures that drive migration.

Promoting Peace and Stability

Promoting peace and stability in the countries of origin for refugees is essential to addressing the root causes of displacement. Many individuals and families flee their homes due to ongoing conflicts, political instability, and economic hardships. By investing in peace-building initiatives, we can create environments where people feel safe and secure, allowing them to remain in their homeland. These initiatives can take various forms, including conflict resolution programs, community dialogue sessions, and support for democratic governance. By fostering an environment conducive to peace, we can significantly reduce the pressures that lead to mass migration.

Economic development is another critical component of promoting stability. Many refugees leave their countries due to a lack of opportunities for employment and education. By supporting sustainable economic growth, we can help communities develop resilience against the factors that drive displacement. This support can come in the form of microfinance programs, vocational training, and investments in local infrastructure. When individuals have access to jobs and education, they are more likely to see a future for themselves and their families in their home countries, reducing the incentive to embark on perilous journeys across the Mediterranean.

In addition to economic support, addressing social inequalities and fostering inclusivity is vital for promoting peace. Marginalized groups, including women and ethnic minorities, often bear the brunt of conflict and instability. By ensuring that all members of society have a voice and the opportunity to participate in decision-making processes, we can build stronger, more cohesive communities. Programs aimed at empowering women and promoting gender equality can lead to significant improvements in societal stability. When everyone feels valued and included, the chances of social unrest diminish.

International cooperation plays a crucial role in promoting peace and stability in regions affected by displacement. Countries must work together to address the transnational nature of many conflicts and crises. This collaboration can take the form of diplomatic efforts, shared intelligence, and coordinated humanitarian responses. By aligning resources and expertise, nations can tackle the complex challenges that drive people from their homes. Furthermore, engaging regional organizations can facilitate dialogue and foster collective approaches to conflict resolution, strengthening the overall stability of the region.

Finally, raising awareness about the importance of promoting peace and stability is essential for mobilizing support for these efforts. Public engagement and education campaigns can help shift perceptions about refugees and highlight the positive contributions they can make to their communities if given the chance. By emphasizing the interconnectedness of global peace and migration issues, we can inspire individuals and organizations to take action. Supporting peace and stability in refugees' homelands is not only a moral imperative but also a practical solution to one of the most pressing challenges of our time.

Chapter 15: International Cooperation and Responsibility

The Role of the United Nations

The United Nations plays a pivotal role in addressing the challenges faced by refugees around the globe, particularly in the context of fostering stability in their home countries. Established to promote international cooperation and peace, the UN has developed a comprehensive framework to support displaced individuals and communities. Through its various agencies, such as the United Nations High Commissioner for Refugees (UNHCR), the organization is dedicated to ensuring the protection of refugees and offering them assistance in rebuilding their lives. This commitment is crucial as it aims to provide solutions that can ultimately reduce the necessity for individuals to undertake perilous journeys across the Mediterranean Sea.

One of the primary functions of the United Nations is to advocate for the rights of refugees and internally displaced persons. The UNHCR, for example, works tirelessly to uphold the principles outlined in the 1951 Refugee Convention, which asserts the right to seek asylum and the obligation of states to protect those who flee persecution. By raising awareness of the plight of refugees and working with governments to implement policies that safeguard their rights, the UN fosters a global environment in which refugees can find safety and support within their own regions. This advocacy is essential in addressing the root causes of displacement, thereby decreasing the likelihood that individuals will feel compelled to leave their countries.

In addition to its advocacy efforts, the United Nations also coordinates humanitarian assistance and development programs aimed at stabilizing countries affected by conflict and crisis. Initiatives funded by the UN provide essential services such as education, healthcare, and vocational training to both refugees and host communities. These programs not only improve the immediate conditions for displaced populations but also contribute to the long-term development of their home countries. By investing in infrastructure and social services, the UN helps create an environment where refugees can envision a future in their homeland, thus reducing the incentive to migrate to Europe or other regions.

Collaboration with local governments and organizations is another critical aspect of the UN's approach to supporting refugees. The UN often works alongside national authorities to develop comprehensive strategies that address the needs of displaced populations while promoting social cohesion. By engaging local communities in the planning and implementation of these strategies, the UN ensures that the solutions are culturally appropriate and sustainable. This collaborative effort is vital in fostering a sense of ownership among local stakeholders, which can lead to more effective and lasting outcomes for refugees and their communities.

Ultimately, the role of the United Nations in supporting refugees extends beyond immediate relief efforts; it encompasses a vision for sustainable solutions that address the underlying causes of displacement. By focusing on policies that promote peace, stability, and development in the home countries of refugees, the UN plays a crucial part in helping individuals find safety and opportunity without having to risk their lives on treacherous journeys. As the international community continues to grapple with the complexities of migration and displacement, the UN's commitment to safeguarding the rights and dignity of refugees remains a cornerstone of efforts to create a more just and equitable world.

Bilateral and Multilateral Agreements

Bilateral and multilateral agreements play a crucial role in shaping the landscape of international relations, particularly in addressing the complexities surrounding refugee movements. These agreements are formal arrangements between two or more states that establish mutual commitments and responsibilities regarding various issues, including the protection of refugees. By fostering cooperation among nations, such agreements can create frameworks that not only facilitate the safe and dignified movement of individuals seeking refuge but also enhance the support mechanisms in their countries of origin. Understanding the significance of these agreements is essential for developing effective strategies to assist refugees and promote stability in their homelands.

Bilateral agreements, typically involving two countries, often focus on specific issues such as repatriation, asylum procedures, and the provision of humanitarian aid. These arrangements can help streamline the process for refugees by clarifying the legal frameworks and responsibilities each country has toward individuals fleeing persecution or conflict. For instance, a bilateral agreement may outline the conditions under which a refugee can return to their home country safely while ensuring that their rights and safety are prioritized. Such frameworks can lead to more effective responses to refugee crises by encouraging collaboration and sharing of best practices between nations.

Multilateral agreements, on the other hand, encompass broader coalitions of countries working together to address shared challenges, including the refugee crisis. These agreements often take the form of international treaties or conventions, such as the 1951 Refugee Convention and its 1967 Protocol. By establishing common standards for the treatment of refugees and the responsibilities of signatory states, multilateral agreements enhance the protection of individuals fleeing conflict and persecution. These frameworks also facilitate the allocation of resources and support, enabling countries to collectively address the root causes of displacement and improve conditions in the refugees' countries of origin.

The effectiveness of bilateral and multilateral agreements in supporting refugees depends significantly on the political will and commitment of the participating nations. When countries prioritize cooperation and shared goals, they can create more robust systems to address the complexities of refugee crises. This commitment can manifest in various forms, such as increased funding for humanitarian assistance, the establishment of safe zones, or initiatives aimed at rebuilding and stabilizing war-torn regions. By focusing on collaborative approaches, nations can foster an environment where refugees are not only protected during their journey but are also supported in their efforts to remain in their home countries.

Ultimately, the success of bilateral and multilateral agreements in supporting refugees hinges on their ability to adapt to changing circumstances and respond to the evolving needs of displaced populations. As global challenges continue to arise, these agreements must remain dynamic and responsive, incorporating new strategies that prioritize the well-being of refugees and their communities. By strengthening international cooperation and fostering dialogue among nations, the potential to create sustainable solutions that enable refugees to stay in their own countries becomes increasingly attainable.

Engaging Non-Governmental Organizations

Engaging non-governmental organizations (NGOs) is a crucial strategy in supporting refugees in their homelands and preventing the perilous journeys many undertake across the Mediterranean Sea to Europe. NGOs often possess the necessary on-the-ground experience, local knowledge, and established relationships with communities that are essential for implementing effective support programs. By collaborating with these organizations, stakeholders can leverage their expertise to create sustainable solutions that address the root causes of forced migration, ensuring that refugees can remain safely in their countries.

The role of NGOs extends beyond immediate humanitarian aid; they are instrumental in advocating for policy changes that improve the conditions for refugees and displaced populations. By working closely with local governments and international bodies, NGOs can influence policies that enhance social services, promote economic development, and protect human rights within refugee-affected regions. This advocacy work is vital in creating an environment where refugees feel secure and empowered, thereby reducing their inclination to migrate under hazardous conditions.

Partnerships with NGOs also facilitate the implementation of various programs aimed at enhancing the quality of life for refugees in their homelands. These programs can include educational initiatives, vocational training, and psychological support services, all of which contribute to building resilience within communities facing displacement. By investing in human capital and providing opportunities for skill development, NGOs can help to create a more stable and hopeful future for refugees, thereby diminishing the factors that lead to migration.

Furthermore, NGOs often serve as a bridge between local communities and larger international entities, ensuring that the voices of refugees are heard and considered in broader discussions about migration and asylum. By engaging in this dialogue, NGOs can highlight the specific needs and challenges faced by refugees, advocating for tailored interventions that address these issues effectively. This grassroots approach ensures that solutions are not only culturally sensitive but also practical and sustainable in the long term.

Finally, fostering strong relationships with NGOs can lead to increased funding opportunities and resource sharing. Collaborative efforts can attract the attention of international donors and foundations interested in supporting refugee initiatives. By pooling resources and expertise, stakeholders can develop comprehensive strategies that enhance the effectiveness of their interventions. This collaborative framework not only strengthens the capacity of NGOs but also amplifies the impact of their work, ultimately contributing to a more robust support system for refugees in their homelands.

Chapter 16: Innovative Solutions for Refugee Support

Technology and Communication

In the contemporary landscape of global migration, technology plays a pivotal role in shaping communication channels for refugees. The proliferation of smartphones and internet access has transformed how individuals in crisis connect with one another and with organizations that offer support. For refugees contemplating perilous journeys, the ability to communicate instantly can provide crucial information about safe routes, available resources, and even the experiences of others who have made similar decisions. This technological connectivity can also foster a sense of community among displaced individuals, who can share their stories and seek solace in shared experiences, even from afar.

Social media platforms have emerged as vital tools for refugees, not just for personal communication but also for mobilizing support. Organizations and activists utilize these platforms to raise awareness about the challenges refugees face, effectively humanizing their plight and encouraging collective action. Through hashtags and viral campaigns, the narratives of refugees can reach a wider audience, compelling individuals and governments to consider policies that support humanitarian efforts. Technology thus serves as a bridge between refugees and potential allies, fostering understanding and empathy that transcends geographic borders.

Moreover, technology facilitates vital access to information that can empower refugees to make informed decisions about their futures. Mobile applications designed for refugees provide critical resources such as legal advice, healthcare services, and educational opportunities. These tools can guide individuals through complex bureaucratic processes, helping them navigate asylum procedures or access emergency assistance. By equipping refugees with knowledge and resources, technology not only aids in their immediate survival but also supports their long-term integration into host communities or their return to safer conditions in their homelands.

Despite these benefits, challenges remain in the realm of technology and communication for refugees. Many refugees face significant barriers to accessing technology, including financial constraints, lack of digital literacy, and limited infrastructure in their regions. Additionally, the digital divide can exacerbate existing inequalities, leaving the most vulnerable populations without critical support. It is essential for humanitarian organizations and governments to address these disparities by providing resources and training that enhance digital access and literacy among refugee populations.

In conclusion, while technology and communication have the potential to significantly enhance the lives of refugees, it is imperative to recognize and address the obstacles that hinder access. Efforts to support refugees must include initiatives that bridge the digital divide, ensuring that all individuals, regardless of their circumstances, can benefit from the advantages that technology offers. By fostering an inclusive approach to technological support, we can enhance the resilience of refugees in their homelands, ultimately contributing to the broader goal of reducing forced migration and empowering communities to thrive in challenging circumstances.

Grassroots Initiatives

Grassroots initiatives play a pivotal role in supporting refugees in their homelands, offering sustainable solutions that address the root causes of displacement. These initiatives often emerge from local communities, harnessing the knowledge and resources of those directly affected by conflict and instability. By focusing on local solutions, grassroots organizations empower individuals and families to rebuild their lives, fostering resilience and stability that can reduce the pressures of migration.

One significant aspect of grassroots initiatives is their ability to adapt to the unique needs of their communities. Local organizations often have a deep understanding of the cultural, social, and economic contexts in which they operate. This knowledge allows them to implement tailored programs that address specific challenges faced by refugees, such as access to education, healthcare, and economic opportunities. By working from within the community, these initiatives can create more effective and sustainable outcomes compared to external interventions that may not fully grasp local dynamics.

Collaboration is another cornerstone of successful grassroots initiatives. By partnering with other local organizations, government entities, and international NGOs, grassroots movements can amplify their impact. These collaborations can facilitate the sharing of resources, knowledge, and best practices, creating a network of support that enhances the overall effectiveness of efforts to assist refugees. Such partnerships can also foster a sense of solidarity and shared responsibility among community members, promoting a collective approach to addressing the challenges faced by displaced populations.

Grassroots initiatives also play a critical role in advocacy and raising awareness about the issues affecting refugees. By sharing stories and highlighting the experiences of those impacted by conflict and displacement, these organizations can influence public opinion and policy. This advocacy work is essential in shifting narratives around refugees, emphasizing their agency and the importance of investing in their homelands. Through campaigns, community events, and social media, grassroots movements can engage a wider audience, mobilizing support for sustainable solutions that keep refugees in their countries.

Ultimately, supporting grassroots initiatives is crucial for creating lasting change in the lives of refugees and their communities. By investing in local solutions, we can foster environments where individuals feel safe, valued, and able to thrive. This approach not only benefits those currently displaced but also contributes to the stability and development of entire regions. As we consider how to effectively address the refugee crisis, it is essential to recognize and empower the grassroots movements that are already making a difference in the lives of countless individuals around the world.

Sustainable Development Goals

Sustainable Development Goals (SDGs) are a universal call to action adopted by the United Nations in 2015, aimed at addressing global challenges and promoting prosperity while protecting the planet. These 17 goals are interconnected and emphasize the need for collaborative approaches to solve issues such as poverty, inequality, climate change, environmental degradation, peace, and justice. For refugees and displaced persons, the SDGs provide a framework that can support efforts to create conditions in their home countries that reduce the need for migration and enhance resilience against the factors that compel them to leave their homes.

One of the most pertinent SDGs in the context of refugees is Goal 1: No Poverty. Many individuals and families flee their countries due to extreme poverty and lack of economic opportunities. By focusing on poverty eradication strategies, governments and organizations can work toward creating sustainable livelihoods that empower communities. Investments in education and vocational training, for instance, can provide individuals with the skills needed to secure decent jobs, thereby reducing economic desperation that often drives migration.

Another crucial goal is Goal 4: Quality Education. Access to quality education is essential for fostering a sense of hope and stability in communities affected by conflict or economic hardship. By prioritizing educational initiatives, countries can help build a knowledgeable and skilled workforce that contributes to social and economic development. This not only benefits individuals but also strengthens communities, making them more resilient to crises and reducing the likelihood of displacement.

Climate action, encapsulated in Goal 13, also plays a significant role in the refugee context. Environmental degradation and climate change are increasingly recognized as drivers of migration. By promoting sustainable agricultural practices, protecting natural resources, and investing in renewable energy, countries can mitigate the impacts of climate change. These actions can help communities adapt to environmental challenges, thereby reducing the pressures that lead to displacement and enabling people to remain in their homes.

Finally, the promotion of peaceful and inclusive societies, as outlined in Goal 16, is vital for addressing the root causes of conflict and instability. Strengthening governance, ensuring access to justice, and fostering inclusive decision-making processes can help build trust within communities. By addressing grievances and promoting dialogue, societies can work toward preventing conflicts that often lead to forced migration. In summary, the Sustainable Development Goals offer a comprehensive roadmap for creating conditions that support refugees in their homelands, highlighting the importance of coordinated efforts to tackle the multifaceted challenges they face.

Chapter 17: The Role of Public Awareness and Advocacy

Media Representation of Refugees

Media representation of refugees plays a crucial role in shaping public perception and influencing policy decisions. The portrayal of refugees in news outlets, documentaries, and social media often frames the narrative around their experiences, challenges, and aspirations. Understanding how these representations affect societal attitudes is essential for fostering a more supportive environment for refugees. Often, media focuses on the dramatic aspects of the refugee crisis, emphasizing perilous journeys across the Mediterranean, which can create a sense of fear or detachment among the audience. This limited perspective can overshadow the multifaceted realities refugees face in their homelands and the potential for support systems that could enable them to remain there.

The sensationalist nature of many media stories often leads to the dehumanization of refugees, reducing individuals to mere statistics or symbols of crisis. This portrayal can perpetuate stereotypes and foster negative attitudes towards refugees, presenting them as burdens rather than as people with unique histories, skills, and contributions to society. In contrast, more balanced media representations that highlight personal stories, resilience, and the cultural richness that refugees bring can enhance empathy and understanding among the public. By sharing the narratives of refugees as individuals with dreams and aspirations, media can challenge prevailing stereotypes and promote a more nuanced view of their situations.

Moreover, media representation can influence public policy and the allocation of resources for refugee assistance. When media coverage emphasizes the humanitarian needs and potential benefits of supporting refugees in their own countries, it can encourage governments and organizations to invest in development initiatives that address the root causes of displacement. This includes focusing on economic stability, education, and healthcare in refugees' home countries, which are critical for reducing the pressures that force individuals to flee. By advocating for a shift from a solely crisis-driven narrative to one that highlights proactive solutions, media can play a pivotal role in shaping more effective and compassionate policies.

The advent of social media has transformed how refugees and their stories are shared and consumed, enabling a more grassroots representation. Refugees themselves can use platforms like Twitter, Instagram, and Facebook to tell their stories, share their experiences, and connect with broader audiences. This direct form of communication can challenge traditional media narratives and provide a more authentic portrayal of refugee lives. However, it also raises the question of responsibility, as the sharing of personal stories can sometimes expose individuals to risks or exploit their vulnerabilities. Thus, it is essential for both traditional and social media to prioritize ethical considerations in their representations of refugees.

Ultimately, the media's role in representing refugees is not just about storytelling; it is about advocacy and accountability. By committing to responsible and accurate representations, media outlets can contribute to a more informed and compassionate public discourse. This, in turn, can lead to a collective understanding of the complexities surrounding the refugee experience and the importance of supporting initiatives that allow individuals to thrive in their own countries. As we navigate the challenges of displacement, it is vital for the media to serve as a bridge between refugees and the public, fostering empathy and encouraging actionable support that transcends borders.

Mobilising Communities for Change

Mobilizing communities for change is a crucial aspect of supporting refugees in their homelands, particularly in the context of the Mediterranean migration crisis. Communities play a vital role in shaping an environment that fosters resilience and sustainability. By engaging local populations, we can create a supportive network that addresses the root causes of displacement. This involves not only raising awareness about the challenges refugees face but also empowering communities to take actionable steps toward improvement. Through collaborative efforts, communities can work together to develop solutions that enhance local conditions, thereby reducing the need for individuals to embark on perilous journeys across the Mediterranean.

A key strategy for mobilizing communities is the promotion of inclusive dialogues that involve all stakeholders, including refugees, local residents, and government officials. These discussions can help identify shared needs and aspirations, fostering a sense of ownership among community members. By facilitating workshops, town hall meetings, and focus groups, we can encourage participation and ensure that diverse voices are heard. Such engagement not only builds trust but also cultivates a collective understanding of the issues at hand. When communities recognize the importance of collaboration, they are more likely to rally around initiatives that support refugees and address local challenges simultaneously.

Education and awareness-raising campaigns are essential components of mobilization efforts. Providing accurate information about the realities of refugee life, the factors driving displacement, and the potential benefits of supporting local integration can shift public perceptions. Community leaders can spearhead these initiatives, leveraging local media, social platforms, and public events to disseminate knowledge. As misconceptions are addressed and empathy is cultivated, community members may become more inclined to participate in efforts that support refugees. This shift in attitude can lead to increased volunteerism, donations, and advocacy for policies that prioritize local solutions over external interventions.

Another vital element in mobilizing communities is the establishment of partnerships with local organizations, NGOs, and international agencies. Collaborations can enhance resource sharing and create a more comprehensive support system for refugees. These partnerships can facilitate training programs, vocational workshops, and access to essential services such as healthcare and legal aid. By pooling resources and expertise, communities can create a robust framework that not only assists refugees but also strengthens local infrastructure. This holistic approach ensures that both refugees and host communities benefit, fostering a more harmonious coexistence.

Finally, it is essential to measure the impact of community mobilization efforts and share successes widely. Documenting stories of change and progress can inspire others and demonstrate the effectiveness of grassroots initiatives. By highlighting successful models of support and integration, we can encourage replication in other regions facing similar challenges. Sharing these narratives creates a ripple effect, motivating communities globally to take action. As communities mobilize for change, they not only uplift refugees but also reinforce their own resilience, ultimately contributing to a more stable and equitable future for all.

The Importance of Education and Empathy

Education and empathy are two critical components in addressing the refugee crisis and fostering sustainable solutions in their homelands. Education serves as a powerful tool for empowerment, enabling individuals to acquire knowledge and skills that can improve their living conditions. In many regions, particularly those affected by conflict or poverty, access to quality education is limited. By investing in educational initiatives, we can provide the youth with the opportunities they need to thrive, reducing the likelihood of them feeling compelled to undertake perilous journeys across borders in search of a better life.

Empathy is equally vital in this context. It allows us to understand the unique challenges faced by refugees and those who remain in their countries of origin. When we cultivate empathy, we create a society that acknowledges the humanity behind the statistics. By recognizing the stories of those affected by displacement, we can better appreciate the complex factors driving migration, such as violence, persecution, and economic instability. This understanding can lead to more compassionate responses from individuals and communities, fostering an environment where constructive dialogues about solutions can take place.

The integration of education and empathy into our approach can lead to innovative solutions that support refugees in their homelands. Educational programs designed with empathy can address specific community needs, providing training in conflict resolution, vocational skills, and entrepreneurship. Such programs empower individuals and communities to rebuild their lives and societies, creating a sense of hope and stability. By equipping refugees with the tools they need, we can help mitigate the conditions that force them to flee, thereby encouraging them to remain in their communities.

Furthermore, promoting education and empathy can lead to stronger social cohesion in host communities. When individuals from different backgrounds engage in educational initiatives that emphasize shared experiences and understanding, they can break down barriers and foster integration. Empathetic education can create opportunities for dialogue between refugees and host communities, dispelling myths and reducing xenophobia. This not only benefits refugees but also enriches the cultural fabric of the host countries, making them more resilient and inclusive.

Ultimately, the importance of education and empathy transcends geographical boundaries. By prioritizing these elements, we can contribute to a more equitable world where refugees are supported in their homelands. This approach fosters a deeper understanding of the root causes of displacement, empowering individuals to change their circumstances. As we work together to create a future where education and empathy flourish, we take significant steps towards addressing the refugee crisis at its source, ensuring that the need for perilous journeys across the Mediterranean diminishes.

Chapter 18: Case Studies

Successful Programs in Conflict Zones

Successful programs in conflict zones demonstrate the potential for empowering communities and reducing the need for forced migration. By addressing the root causes of conflict and instability, these initiatives can create environments where individuals and families feel safe and supported. One prominent example is the work of non-governmental organizations (NGOs) that focus on educational initiatives. Providing access to quality education not only equips children with essential skills but also fosters a sense of normalcy and hope amidst chaos. Programs that train local teachers and develop curricula relevant to the challenges faced in conflict zones help to sustain educational efforts even when resources are scarce.

Economic development initiatives also play a critical role in stabilizing conflict-affected regions. Programs that promote entrepreneurship and provide microloans enable individuals to start their businesses, generating income and employment opportunities. These economic interventions can help communities become self-sufficient, reducing dependency on external aid and fostering resilience. For example, in regions affected by prolonged conflict, initiatives that support women entrepreneurs have shown significant promise. By empowering women, these programs not only contribute to economic growth but also challenge gender norms and promote social cohesion.

Healthcare programs in conflict zones are essential for ensuring the well-being of displaced populations. Initiatives that provide mobile clinics or telemedicine services can reach those who are often cut off from traditional healthcare facilities. By addressing both physical and mental health needs, these programs help to restore dignity and improve the overall quality of life for affected communities. For instance, partnerships between local health workers and international organizations can enhance the capacity of healthcare systems, ensuring that even in the most challenging circumstances, individuals receive the care they need.

Community-based peacebuilding programs are another successful approach in conflict zones. These initiatives focus on fostering dialogue and reconciliation among diverse groups, promoting social cohesion and reducing tensions. By involving local leaders and community members, peacebuilding efforts can cultivate trust and understanding, essential elements for long-term stability. For example, programs that create safe spaces for dialogue have been effective in mitigating violence and encouraging collaboration among different ethnic or religious groups. Such initiatives not only address immediate conflicts but also lay the groundwork for sustainable peace.

Lastly, leveraging technology in conflict zones has emerged as a powerful tool for driving change. Innovative solutions such as mobile apps for reporting safety concerns or online platforms for education can significantly enhance the reach and impact of humanitarian efforts. By utilizing technology, organizations can provide timely information and resources to those in need, bridging gaps created by conflict. Successful programs that incorporate technology demonstrate that even in the most challenging environments, creative solutions can lead to significant improvements in the lives of refugees and displaced individuals, ultimately contributing to a more stable and hopeful future in their homelands.

Examples of Effective Local Initiatives

Local initiatives play a crucial role in addressing the challenges faced by refugees in their homelands. By focusing on the specific needs of communities, these initiatives foster resilience and provide support that enables individuals to remain in their countries rather than feeling compelled to embark on dangerous journeys. One example of such an initiative is the establishment of community-based agriculture programs in regions affected by conflict and displacement. These programs not only provide food security but also empower refugees and local populations through skills training and access to markets. By cultivating crops and livestock, participants can generate income, thus reducing the economic pressures that often lead to migration.

Another effective local initiative is the creation of educational programs tailored for refugee children. In areas with a high influx of displaced families, local organizations have developed makeshift schools that offer curricula aligned with national education standards. These schools are staffed by volunteers from the community, many of whom are also refugees. By ensuring that children receive an education, these initiatives help to break the cycle of poverty and give families a reason to stay in their homeland. Additionally, these educational programs often incorporate psychosocial support, addressing the trauma that many children have experienced due to conflict, thus fostering a sense of normalcy and hope for the future.

Healthcare access is another critical area where local initiatives have made significant strides. In many regions, local NGOs have set up mobile clinics that reach underserved communities, including refugees. These clinics provide essential medical services, vaccinations, and maternal health care, which are vital for families who may feel isolated and neglected by the formal healthcare system. By addressing health disparities, these initiatives not only improve the quality of life for refugees but also strengthen community resilience, making it less likely that families will consider leaving their homes in search of better healthcare opportunities.

Moreover, local initiatives that focus on vocational training and employment opportunities have proven essential in supporting refugees' integration into their communities. Programs that offer skills development in areas such as carpentry, tailoring, and technology enable refugees to gain employment and contribute economically to their local economies. For instance, partnerships between local businesses and refugee organizations can create job opportunities that benefit both parties. By investing in the skills of refugees, communities foster a culture of inclusion and cooperation, which can help to alleviate tensions that sometimes arise from the arrival of displaced populations.

Lastly, advocacy and awareness-raising initiatives play a pivotal role in changing perceptions about refugees and their contributions to society. Local campaigns that highlight success stories of refugees who have become integral members of their communities can shift public opinion and encourage support for policies that aid in their integration. These initiatives often involve collaborations between local governments, civil society, and the private sector, creating a united front in the effort to enhance the lives of refugees. By showcasing the positive impact of refugees, these campaigns not only foster empathy but also encourage the community to take a stand against xenophobia and discrimination, ultimately promoting a more inclusive society where everyone can thrive.

Lessons Learned from Global Practices

Understanding the challenges faced by refugees requires a comprehensive examination of global practices in humanitarian support and development. Several countries have implemented innovative strategies that have proven effective in addressing the root causes of displacement. For instance, countries like Jordan and Lebanon have adopted policies that integrate refugees into local economies and communities, providing them with access to education, healthcare, and job opportunities. These practices demonstrate the importance of fostering inclusive environments where refugees can contribute to society rather than being seen solely as a burden.

One significant lesson learned from these global practices is the necessity of collaboration between governments, non-governmental organizations, and local communities. In many cases, successful initiatives have emerged from partnerships that leverage the strengths of various stakeholders. For example, in Uganda, the government has embraced a progressive refugee policy that allows refugees to own land and start businesses. This collaboration has not only improved the lives of refugees but has also stimulated local economies and fostered social cohesion. The Ugandan model highlights the importance of a holistic approach that engages all sectors of society in the support of refugees.

Education emerges as another critical area where lessons can be drawn from global practices. Countries that have prioritized educational access for refugees have seen positive outcomes in terms of integration and long-term stability. For instance, in Germany, language and vocational training programs have been implemented to help refugees assimilate into the workforce. These educational initiatives have proven essential in enabling refugees to rebuild their lives and contribute to their host communities. The emphasis on education underscores the need for targeted interventions that empower refugees with the skills necessary for self-sufficiency.

Furthermore, addressing the root causes of displacement is vital in the quest to support refugees in their homelands. Global practices have shown that effective responses to conflict, climate change, and economic instability can significantly reduce the number of people forced to flee their homes. For instance, development programs aimed at improving infrastructure and governance in conflict-prone regions have resulted in decreased migration pressures. By investing in stability and resilience within countries of origin, the international community can help create conditions that allow individuals to remain in their home countries and thrive.

Finally, the importance of cultural sensitivity and community engagement cannot be overstated. Successful global practices have often incorporated the voices and needs of refugees themselves, ensuring that support programs are tailored to their unique circumstances. Initiatives that involve refugees in decision-making processes not only enhance the effectiveness of aid but also empower individuals to take ownership of their futures. This approach fosters a sense of agency among refugees, reinforcing the idea that they are active participants in their development rather than passive recipients of aid. By learning from these global practices, we can develop more effective strategies to support refugees and ultimately help them to stay in their own countries.

Chapter 19: Moving Forward

Strategies for Long-Term Support

Long-term support for refugees is essential in creating sustainable solutions that encourage individuals to remain in their homelands. One effective strategy involves empowering local communities through education and vocational training. By investing in educational initiatives that are accessible to displaced individuals, we can equip them with the skills necessary to generate income and contribute to their local economies. This not only benefits the individuals but also strengthens the community as a whole, fostering resilience and reducing the likelihood of further displacement.

Another critical strategy is enhancing local infrastructure and services. In many cases, refugees return to or remain in areas that lack adequate healthcare, sanitation, and housing. By collaborating with governments and NGOs, we can direct resources toward improving these essential services. This approach not only addresses the immediate needs of refugees but also improves the quality of life for the entire population, thereby creating a more stable environment conducive to long-term residency.

Economic development plays a vital role in supporting refugees in their home countries. Initiatives that promote entrepreneurship and small business development can provide refugees with opportunities to establish their livelihoods. By offering microloans, grants, and training programs, we can help individuals start businesses that serve their communities. This not only generates income but also fosters a sense of purpose and belonging, which is crucial for mental well-being in the aftermath of displacement.

Building strong networks of support within communities is also essential. Engaging local populations in the integration process can help mitigate tensions and foster understanding between refugees and host communities. By promoting dialogue and collaboration, we can create an atmosphere of mutual respect and solidarity. Support groups and community events can facilitate connections and provide platforms for shared experiences, ultimately leading to a more cohesive society.

Lastly, advocating for policy changes that protect the rights of refugees is crucial for long-term support. Engaging with policymakers to promote inclusive legislation can ensure that refugees have access to essential services and employment opportunities. Additionally, raising awareness about the contributions of refugees to their communities can shift public perception and encourage a supportive environment. By combining advocacy with grassroots initiatives, we can create a comprehensive approach that not only addresses the immediate needs of refugees but also lays the groundwork for a stable future in their home countries.

Building Resilience in Refugee Communities

Building resilience in refugee communities is crucial for empowering individuals and families to cope with the challenges they face. Resilience refers to the ability to adapt to adversity, recover from setbacks, and continue to thrive despite difficulties. In the context of refugee communities, fostering resilience involves not only addressing immediate needs but also enhancing long-term capacities that allow individuals to rebuild their lives. This multifaceted approach recognizes the importance of social, economic, and psychological resources that enable refugees to navigate their circumstances effectively.

One of the primary ways to build resilience in refugee communities is through educational initiatives. Access to quality education can provide refugees with the skills and knowledge necessary to improve their livelihoods and integrate into society. Programs that focus on language acquisition, vocational training, and cultural orientation can help refugees become active participants in their communities. Additionally, educational initiatives should involve the local population to promote mutual understanding and cooperation, reducing tensions and fostering a sense of belonging.

Economic empowerment is another critical component of building resilience. Providing refugees with access to microfinance, job training, and entrepreneurship opportunities can help them establish sustainable livelihoods. By creating pathways to employment, refugees can gain financial independence and contribute to their local economies. Collaborative efforts between governments, NGOs, and private sectors are essential in developing programs that support job creation and skills development tailored to the specific needs of refugee communities.

Mental health support plays a vital role in fostering resilience among refugees. Many individuals face trauma from violence, loss, and displacement, which can have long-lasting effects on their well-being. Integrating mental health services into community programs can help address these issues by providing counseling, support groups, and psychosocial interventions. Building a network of support within the community encourages individuals to share their experiences and seek help, which is essential for healing and rebuilding trust.

Finally, promoting social cohesion and community engagement is integral to resilience building. Encouraging refugees to participate in community activities and decision-making processes can strengthen social networks and promote a sense of ownership. Initiatives that facilitate cultural exchange and collaboration between refugees and host communities can help break down barriers and foster mutual respect. By cultivating an inclusive environment, we can empower refugees to overcome challenges and contribute positively to their communities, ultimately enhancing their resilience and capacity to thrive.

The Future of Migration and Refugee Policy

The future of migration and refugee policy is poised for significant transformation as global dynamics shift and the need for compassionate responses becomes ever more urgent. Policymakers and humanitarian organizations are increasingly recognizing that effective solutions require a multi-faceted approach that addresses not only the immediate needs of refugees but also the underlying factors that drive migration. In this context, understanding the complex interplay between economic, political, and environmental pressures is essential for developing policies that can provide support to individuals in their home countries, thereby mitigating the need for perilous journeys across the Mediterranean Sea.

One of the most critical aspects of future migration policy is the emphasis on creating conditions that allow individuals to thrive in their own communities. This involves investing in local economies, enhancing educational opportunities, and improving access to healthcare. By fostering sustainable development, countries can provide their citizens with the tools and resources necessary to build stable lives at home. Strengthening local governance and promoting the rule of law are also pivotal, as these factors contribute to a more secure environment that diminishes the motivation for individuals to leave their homes in search of safety and opportunity abroad.

International collaboration will play a vital role in shaping effective migration and refugee policies. Countries must work together to share best practices, resources, and knowledge, particularly in regions that are heavily impacted by migration flows. The establishment of partnerships between donor nations and countries experiencing high levels of outmigration can facilitate the implementation of programs aimed at improving socio-economic conditions. Additionally, fostering dialogue among nations can lead to harmonized policies that protect the rights of refugees and migrants while ensuring that host countries can manage integration processes effectively.

Moreover, addressing the root causes of forced migration requires a comprehensive understanding of global issues such as climate change, conflict, and economic inequality. Future policies must prioritize resilience-building initiatives that prepare communities for the challenges posed by environmental degradation and socio-political instability. Investment in climate adaptation strategies and conflict resolution mechanisms can significantly reduce the number of individuals who feel compelled to flee their homes. By proactively engaging with these challenges, the international community can help create a more stable and secure future for vulnerable populations.

Finally, it is crucial to involve refugees and migrants themselves in the policymaking process. Their lived experiences and insights can provide invaluable guidance for developing effective and compassionate policies. Engaging with affected communities ensures that their needs and aspirations are reflected in the solutions devised. By placing refugees at the center of the conversation, policymakers can create a more inclusive and equitable framework that not only addresses the immediate needs of those seeking refuge but also paves the way for a future where individuals can remain in their homelands safely and with dignity.